7

RULES

YOU WERE
BORN TO

BREAK

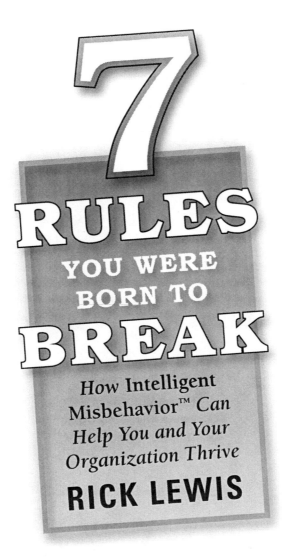

7 RULES

YOU WERE BORN TO

BREAK

How Intelligent Misbehavior™ Can Help You and Your Organization Thrive

RICK LEWIS

Break a Rule Publishing

Vancouver, BC, Canada

ISBN 978-0-9866730-0-9

COVER DESIGN
Kim Johansen – **Black Dog Design**
www.blackdogdesign.com

INTERIOR LAYOUT
Kim Johansen – **Black Dog Design**
Zachary Parker – **Kadak Graphics**

Printed in the United States of America

The term **Intelligent Misbehavior** has been trademarked by Rick Lewis, though it is used throughout this book without the "TM" mark accompanying each appearance of the phrase.

BREAK A RULE PUBLISHING
PO Box 102 – 4438 W 10th Ave.
Vancouver, BC V6R 4R8

This book is dedicated to all intelligent misbehavers

—past, present and future—

who remind us of what life can be.

Contents

Preface

HAVING HAD SOME TRAINING as a magician as well as a comedian and circus performer, I want to tell you a secret that I learned about how magicians fool us.

It works like this.

Imagine that the magician removes a small red scarf from his pocket. He holds it up for us to see and then tells us what he's about to do. He says, "I'm going to place this scarf inside my hand, then I'm going to count to three, and by the time I open my hand, the scarf will be gone." In the meantime, he has stuffed the scarf into his fist.

Then he says, "Now pay attention, because if you're not watching carefully, you're going to be fooled." He implies that if we concentrate on what he's doing, we'll be able to figure out the trick. We may even feel empowered because we've been given a warning and the opportunity to save ourselves from being deceived.

The trick we're hoping to catch, however, has already happened. The scarf is long gone from the magician's fist before he invites us to start paying attention. In our naiveté, we believe that the magician is giving us a sporting chance. I'm sorry to say it, but no, he isn't.

This is an exact metaphor for what is currently happening in our daily lives. On the stage of real life, it is our cultural conditioning that takes the place of the magician. As hard as we try to watch carefully, most of us keep getting tricked into compromising our vision of excellence. That's because the unwritten rules of our culture have already happened. They were introduced to us early in our lives, and they now have an influence on us that we don't even see. By the time we start thinking about realizing a personal vision or dream, we've already been stripped of our potential.

Usually, when a magician performs a trick, it's better not to know how he does it, since the feeling of mystery is so much more satisfying than understanding how it's done. It's one thing to have a quarter disappear before our eyes—entirely another when half our life savings disappears. When important things go missing, we have a right to straight answers. If our joy, enthusiasm, fulfillment, and delight are nowhere to be found, we deserve to know what happened.

Before becoming a corporate presenter I street performed for almost twenty years. A street show is a micromodel for organizational growth. It is interactive, and, as in any business, nothing happens without the active participation of others. The street entertainer, like the business manager, must have strong relationship skills, engender trust and confidence in his or her audience, and inspire others to action. To do that, he or she has to deeply understand the things that stop us.

This book is about seven rules that we unconsciously obey and that stop us from taking positive action. The obstacles that prevent an entertainer from building a successful show are the same as those that prevent organizations from thriving. In this book I share strategies for individual and group success that I learned while performing on the street and while entertaining the leaders and executives who run our largest companies.

The best thing we can do in support of any organization we care about is to encourage the development and progress of its members. As you are about to read, however, there are some unaddressed obstacles that lie between excellence and us. When these hidden obstacles are properly understood and managed, both individuals and the organizations they work for experience dramatic benefits.

The primary focus of any organization is to remain true to its core vision and purpose. Today we face many significant challenges in all of our organizations, from families to neighborhoods, from businesses to governments, and from nations to the global community. While this book doesn't pretend to address the full complexity of those challenges, it is meant to spark a fresh conversation about where excellence really comes from and how it can be sustained.

Introduction

I'VE MADE A LIVING AS A JUGGLER, actor, comedian, and variety entertainer for the last thirty years. The first phase of my career involved performing on the street for donations, which I did while traveling throughout the US, Canada, New Zealand, Australia, and China.

A vice president of marketing for General Electric Corporation "discovered" me at a street performers' festival when I was in my thirties. He invited me to perform for an event GE was holding in Tampa, Florida.

One day I was rolling dimes and quarters from my donation hat into coin wrappers and taking them to the bank to deposit for rent. The next I was on a plane to Florida, taken in a limo to a posh, upscale resort, and shown to a room that had its own spa, bar, and patio overlooking the pool. A far cry from the street, here I would have at my beck and call an entire production team dedicated to providing me with whatever lighting, sound and staging I would need to entertain my audience.

I was happy but also quite nervous, as I wondered if I could live up to the expectations of this corporate executive and adjust to an event of this caliber. My street show depended upon audience participation for its success and involved direct and spontaneous interactions with my crowd. It was designed to have an edge that challenged the boundaries of standard behavior. The corporate environment, in contrast, involves observing clearly defined protocols, roles, and hierarchies—not participating in their breakdown.

I spent the night prior to the performance anxiously trying to figure out how to modify my street show to play to five hundred GE management executives who had come from all over the world for this meeting. I imagined what would or wouldn't be acceptable to them and started editing my standard presentation according to my guesses about what they would tolerate.

The next morning I got up early and headed toward the ballroom, where preparations for the evening event were already under way. I spent the day coordinating with the technical crews: establishing cues, timing, sound levels and presentation details that would assure everything went off according to plan.

When the ballroom doors finally opened, I watched the attendees file in. They were finely groomed, self-assured, obviously intelligent, multilingual, and well-off. I had a detailed picture in my mind as to how I was going to adapt the broad slapstick of my street show to the conventions of this crowd. I repeated it in my head right up until it was time to go on at the end of their meal.

When the emcee finally announced my name and I set foot on stage, the extensive plans for how I was going to provide these corporate executives with what they expected vanished. Once I was in front of the crowd I instinctively turned to the one main thing that had been the basis of my success as an entertainer.

Breaking rules.

A single street show could include rummaging through a woman's purse, sampling the food of passing shoppers without their permission, stopping traffic in the middle of the road, and coaxing reluctant volunteers on stage to help me. Added to this mix were the throwing of sharp objects into the air, stealing the watches of audience members without their knowledge, and at the end asking for money from people I had never met. I'd cross lines and break rules that under other circumstances could have resulted in jail time; yet, in the context of my performance, people loved it and paid me for it. In short, I had become a professional misbehaver.

What the GE executive saw on the street and had appreciated enough to fly me in for his event was the fun and power of rule breaking—an ability to dance on the lines of social order in a way that others found both hilarious and liberating. My show was a public celebration of misbehavior.

This is how I came to abandon my careful plan seconds from making my debut on the corporate stage and instead launch into the show I was meant to do. I delivered what had worked in every market, in every alley, and on every street corner where I had ever drawn a crowd. The production folks scrambled to follow the show as the "stage" expanded to include the entire room, while the audience ate it up. I discovered that day just how hungry these refined guests also were for the fun of rule breaking.

When I returned home I immediately began getting spin-off offers from executives of other companies and the meeting professionals who had been involved with the event.

Since then I've provided a unique brand of comedy for events attended by the Clintons, the Prime Minister of Canada, the Canadian ambassador to the US, Bill Gates, the international board of MasterCard, and countless upper management teams for Fortune 500 companies all over North America.

I've appeared on programs like *Good Morning America* and *America's Funniest People* and performed for individuals who run the financial, pharmaceutical, insurance, and hospitality industries throughout North America. I've also continued to perform on the streets. This makes me a privileged person—not from the standpoint of luxuries but in perspective. I have an equal view of the dirt floor and the red carpet. From passing a hat on street corners to the banquet halls of the corporate elite, I've witnessed a great deal of the diversity of our world. At the same time that I've been making a living entertaining people for the last several decades, I've also become an accidental sociologist.

What I've noticed is that we are all culturally bound by a set of hidden rules regardless of how much we make, what we do, or where we live. We've collectively adopted limitations that divest us of the power, joy, clarity, and purpose with which we were born to live.

My experience working with so many people has made our strengths as well as our limitations apparent. I've seen that the human spirit in each of us never goes away, no matter how buried it might get beneath layers of cultural injunctions and obstacles. We are essentially good and we have an innate potential for excellence. Much more than we'll usually admit. We long to grow, to create, and to bring value to others. We want to rise above challenges and to fulfill our highest purpose. Yet, many of us feel confused or even bewildered by what seem to be invisible forces that stop us from reaching our goals. I'm about to reveal exactly what those forces are, and you may be surprised when you discover how seven simple, accepted, everyday ideas are stopping us from living the lives we dream of.

When I refer to "the lives we dream of" I'm not talking about perpetually lounging on a beach on a tropical island, winning a million dollar lottery jackpot, or finding the absolutely perfect mate. Those are not dreams, they're fantasies. True dreams have heart, and their fulfillment always involves freeing ourselves to be able to make the unique contribution to the world that we were born to provide. Deep down we know that we ought to be experimenting, participating, risking, making mistakes, and going after the possibilities that call to us. We know we should be challenging anything that prevents us from pursuing our highest aspirations—from actualizing our personal visions of what we could offer to this world if we were unhesitant in action, unapologetic in attitude, and confident in spirit.

This is what I offer: a street-level, practically oriented, example-driven guide to reclaiming excellence that is based on the necessity of rule breaking and the wisdom of **Intelligent Misbehavior.**

Intelligent Misbehavior is the willingness to challenge
the hidden rules in our culture that compromise
individual and organizational potential.

Here you will find real-life stories that will illustrate the seven
unspoken rules that silently imprison us and the **Actions of
Intelligent Misbehavior** (AIMs) that can liberate us. As you are
about to see, I've been encouraged by the example of others who
have stood up to these rules. At other times, I've been sobered
by the ways we so quickly cave in to them.

Breaking hidden rules is the domain of the comedian: to go
right to the heart of what is taboo and to release our tension
through laughter. While I love entertaining others, I enjoy even
more inspiring them to rise above the paralysis and confusion
that is brought on by our hidden rules. There has been nothing
more satisfying than seeing withdrawal and indifference be trans-
formed into participation and enjoyment.

If we truly desire excellence, we must make an intentional
choice to misbehave.

Let's break some rules!

1

BE NORMAL

....

I'M A COLLEGE DROPOUT AND I've been divorced. I didn't lose my virginity until I was twenty-one. When I was a child I wanted to be a mime when I grew up. I once invested ten thousand dollars in an oil well I never saw, and lost it all. I wet the bed until I was ten years old because I was too scared to walk out into the dark hallway at night. I never partied as a teenager. I was too busy in my backyard teaching myself how to juggle to spend time seeking acceptance from my peers.

I was not a normal child, and neither were you, yet you and I have both been conditioned to "be normal" when in public.

The upshot of this is that we all have split personalities. We have the persona we put on in public like a school uniform that allows us to fit in, while on the inside we have Shirley Temple with her tap shoes on and Jim Nabors ready to sing.

When a stand-up comedian talks about the human idiosyncrasies, thoughts and habits that we've been trained to keep secret and private, we find delight, and we laugh. A new door is opened for us as we're reminded that authenticity is an option. We don't have to hide who we really are. We can accept ourselves, share our humanity, and stand out as we are.

Under certain specific circumstances fitting in is the intelligent thing to do. If you're a traveler who is visiting a locale populated by thieves, it's not a good idea to dress and behave like a tourist. While blending in is sometimes a wise choice, habitually conforming to the expectations of our environment can gradually lead us away from our authentic visions, goals and priorities.

Normal is getting dressed in clothes that you buy for work and driving through traffic in a car that you're still paying for in order to get to the job you need to pay for the clothes and the car and the house you leave vacant all day so you can afford to live in it.

—Ellen DeGeneres

The problem with always fitting in and adapting ourselves to what we think others will like or accept is that we lose contact with the very basis of our chance to excel. As human beings we are unique and distinct. The wholehearted expression of our differences is the value we bring to the world.

THE FIRST ACTION OF **INTELLIGENT MISBEHAVIOR** IS:

Be Authentic

Defying Expectations

While I have had a great deal of experience performing as a street entertainer and in all kinds of alternative settings over the years, most of my presentations these days take place at corporate events.

Many of these events have a meal associated with them. Instead of just showing up on stage as a comedian, I begin the function playing a character I call the World's Funniest Waiter. The routine centers around the ways in which we expect each other to fit in and what happens when we behave outside of normal patterns and do things our own way. The inspiration for the routine came from my observation of the narrowly defined behavior that is expected from a waiter.

To fit in, I dress identically to the serving staff at the venue where I will be performing. I then show up at the event pretending to be an ordinary staff member, circulate through the room in uniform, attend to water glasses, and look busy in all the usual ways. The guests have no idea that I'm an entertainer.

Over the course of the meal, however, my actions become

increasingly eccentric. I don't touch their food, spill anything, or cause any harm. It's not a rude waiter routine. I'll fill a guest's glass by trickling water slowly into it from my pitcher held two feet above the glass until the water is literally bulging over the rim. I might pocket rolls from the buffet, ask diners if they're done when they've only just received their meals, or crawl under a table to retrieve fallen silverware. It is a portrayal of oddity, of obliviousness to normal and expected behavior.

By the end of the meal, many of the guests have whispered to the person next to them, "Did you just see what I saw?"

The server's job is to blend, stay out of the way, get the people who are paying the bill what they want, and otherwise remain in the background. In the scheme of things, a little eccentric table service is a minor breach of routine. The reactions and responses of the dinner guests when I break these unwritten rules, however, demonstrate our fierce dependency on standard scripts of behavior. In the course of a meal, I'm routinely the recipient of sideways glances, dirty looks, and outright glowering stares. Some people are left with their mouths hanging open, wanting to say something but not knowing where to begin. Others giggle nervously. Still others simply laugh, instinctively appreciative of some relief from the ordinary.

At conferences oriented around sales or performance improvement trainings I've had attendees pull me aside and use their freshly acquired relationship-building and communication techniques to help me see the shortcomings of my service. When I first began doing this routine, I had two other servers at one five-star hotel escort me out of the room after I had asked the guests at a table to pass their dirty plates around the table to me rather than bothering to collect them. Now I always meet with the service staff prior to the event and explain what I've been hired to do.

Years ago I was hired by an association in the Pacific Northwest to perform this act for three hundred professionals in the field of mental health. By the end of the meal, most of the assembled guests had formed a clinical diagnosis for my condition. They weren't saying it out loud, but the professional opinion was thick in the air.

Toward the end of the meal I intentionally tripped over a tray of metal plate warmers, the covers that get used to keep meals warm in a banquet hall until they're served. Think Chevy Chase in a server's outfit.

I was making a production of getting myself off the ground and collecting the metal covers. One of the guests, who had been watching me carefully throughout the evening from a nearby table, leapt out of his seat, came to where I was sprawled on the floor, and picked me up. I noticed right away that he had a very tight grip on my arm.

He swung me around to face him and made very deliberate eye contact with me. "Are you okay?" he asked forcefully.

It was a moment frozen in time. Everything had come to a complete halt in the ballroom, and the rest of the guests had gone silent while watching us. "Yeah, I'm okay," I responded quietly.

He said, "Are you sure? That was a pretty bad fall. Do you want to come over and sit down for a minute?" The words were kind, courteous, and considerate, but the underlying tone made it clear that he considered me to be, as the expression goes, "a couplet short of a sonnet."

He was clearly functioning in a professional capacity and had already drawn some conclusions about my state. This was somewhat alarming to me so I tried to counter, again quietly, by looking at him with a very level expression, hoping that his professional discrimination would allow him to see how lucid I actually was. I repeated, "*Really*, I'm okay."

I thought he had understood until he said, "Well, you may feel okay, but I think it might be a good idea if you and I went for a little walk."

Fearing that I was about to be placed in a headlock, I dropped my character completely and decided to just tell him the truth without subtlety. I could sense that I had only a small window of opportunity left to convince this man of the reality of the situation. Hoping no one else in the room would hear as they looked on, I spoke to him in a sincere and straightforward way. "I'm a *performer*," I said. "I've been hired by your association management to do a comedy show. I'm about to go onstage and start a juggling routine."

There was a long pause as my words hung between us. I waited for him to release his grip. Instead, he looked even more deeply into my eyes, tightened his hold on my arm, and said, "I understand. Come with me."

Fortunately, the woman who had booked me through the association's administrative department was realizing that something was up. She left her seat and approached us giggling, trying to suppress outright laughter. "Excuse me," she said politely. "I hired this man. He's our entertainer."

The fellow finally released his grip at that point. He lowered his hands to his side and just looked at me with an expression that would have been appropriate to his having been told at the age of sixty that he was not the natural-born son of his parents. He could not reconcile the truth of the circumstance with his previous professional assessment of it.

I had been hired by a group whose professional focus involves the defining of "normal" behavior. My would-be helper's actions are quite standard for our culture. We generally try to eliminate differences in others and bring them into line when they're doing things their own way, as though something is wrong with them. When we sacrifice our own authenticity, we most often wind up wanting those around us to remain bound by the same limitations of expression and behavior.

Any form of excellence is a bold expression of how we differ from others and makes us stand out as an example of distinct accomplishment. We arrive there by having found our own way and by leaving normal expectations behind.

Any time we muster the courage to defy expectations we're going to run into resistance from others who have an investment in normal patterns. If we are willing to ignore the opinions of the normal world as we move beyond our habits, what we find on the other side is a whole new vista of possibilities and potential.

Doing What We Love

At fifteen years of age I had no doubt about my interests. I loved being in front of a crowd, entertaining people, and making them laugh. I had been performing for a number of years—acting in stage plays, putting on neighborhood shows, and especially practicing pantomime routines.

At the time, we lived in a suburb of Milwaukee, Wisconsin. One year the city of Milwaukee announced a citywide talent competition. I was anxious for any opportunity to get on stage, and my parents helped me sign up. I entered as a classic mime in whiteface and prepared a series of pantomime skits.

There was a preliminary local competition, which I won, and the finals were to be held in the public band shell of the city's Humboldt Park a few weeks later. I practiced my routines over and over, not set on winning against the talent from the rest of the entire city's population, just excited about being on stage.

The day of the finals arrived, and I remember nervously pacing in the wings as a collection of young performers one by one took their places on stage before the judges to display their skills and talents.

I recall feeling completely outclassed by my performing peers. They were dressed in classy outfits, presented themselves in a poised manner, and spoke with eloquence. Many were musicians who had evidently been trained to present at recitals and other competitions. I especially remember a cello player and a classical pianist who appeared exceptionally skilled to me. I was daunted by these competitors—until I got on stage. What took over once I had the stage all to myself was the enthusiasm of doing what I loved to do. My silent comedy routines were distinct from anything that was being offered by the other contestants. I relished any opportunity to ham it up, sell a gag, and make an audience erupt with laughter.

We were all brought onstage at the end, and the judges began to announce the winners in each of several categories, leaving the announcement of the overall winner to the end. After fifth, fourth, and third places had been announced, my spirits fell, as I felt sure that the judges had overlooked my efforts. Second place was announced, and I still had not been acknowledged.

What I most remember when they called my name for first place and the overall win of the competition was the look of incredulity on the part of those same seasoned, refined, and experienced teen contestants. I feel certain to this day that focusing on what I was truly passionate about rather than trying to do "classy" better was what tipped the judges in my favor. I was in innocent and unbridled pursuit of what I loved and was meant to do.

We are trained, unfortunately, to be normal and to hide our differences, not explore and celebrate them. We need courage to excel, since there will always be those who try to keep us in line by calling us a show-off. As we honor our authentic expression more consistently, such threats will no longer stop us from shining.

Being Spontaneous

A few years ago I was traveling home the day after a performance and speaking engagement for the Executive Club of Louisville in Kentucky. Tornado warnings and high winds delayed my small plane from departing from Louisville on schedule. Hours later we finally landed on the runway in Charlotte, North Carolina, with just enough time for me to make my connection to Phoenix. But as we reached the end of the runway after touch-down, the plane's brakes promptly locked, and we sat immobile for an hour while we waited for a maintenance crew to tow us in. It was just one of those days.

The forty-five minute layover I was supposed to have before my final flight became a butt-numbing eight-hour wait in the Charlotte terminal. On top of that, I missed my ride home on the other end and had a further wait in the Phoenix airport before catching the last shuttle of the day. Weary from the day's events, I dragged my bags off the carousel and pulled them aside, opening one of them to get a toothbrush. I had to take out a number of things to reach it. I put everything else away and headed for the men's room with my bags in tow.

As I was brushing my teeth, two other travelers entered the lavatory and stood on either side of me, fussing with their hair in an odd way. I left and they left.

I headed for the elevators to ascend to the departure level for food. The same men who were in the bathroom boarded the elevator behind me, taking places in the two back corners. When I exited the elevator, they followed, and as I turned into the empty corridor leading toward the food court, they passed me briskly, flanking me on both sides, then quickly pivoted in front of me, blocking my path. One of them whipped out a shiny metal badge that he flashed before my nose and curtly introduced himself as an officer with the Department of Homeland Security.

It turns out that opening and digging through my luggage adjacent to the carousel was not a normal thing to do. Since it was suspicious behavior, the officers started asking a lot of questions, the final one being, "How do we know these bags are yours?"

I started fumbling for the bag claim stubs that were still stapled to my boarding pass sleeve and while pulling it out remembered that I had removed the actual routing tags and tossed them in the trash when I first took possession of my bags.

I had, in fact, no way of proving the luggage was mine.

I suddenly had an idea. I opened up my prop case and pulled out a few things that any non-owner would be unlikely to know what to do with. There in the airport the officers found themselves audience to an impromptu five-minute version of my variety show, with juggling balls, clubs, and other assorted objects being tossed and balanced in the air in front of them. Their undercover tough-cop exteriors melted immediately, and they broke into gales of laughter. They apologized profusely and told me that I had made their last four-month stint in the airport worth it. They walked away as relaxed human beings instead of cold authority figures.

Each of the seven rules, including the rule *be normal*, invites us to forget who we really are and to take part in a rule-script that disconnects us from our potential. When we try to pretend that we're just like everyone else, we separate ourselves from the reality of the moment and the kind of spontaneity that stands out as an expression of freedom, joy, and excellence. If we can relax and remember the option of playfulness when a rule-script has been set in motion, we can often step outside of its influence.

Communication

When an organization is infected by the rule *be normal*, free expression is shut down and communication suffers. Our honest feelings, perspectives, and opinions always defy expectations because we are each unique. This is why people who are authentic are so refreshing. The more we allow ourselves to do what we love and act spontaneously, the closer we come to the truth of our authentic experience. Communication channels open when the members of any group take the initiative to express their experiences openly, as long as that communication is made in a responsible manner.

I recently presented at a year-end party for a very successful family-owned business that supplies medical transport to remote areas of the southwestern states. After having worked with a number of their employees over a period of weeks on the logistical arrangements for the function, I noticed how happy these folks were. At the event itself, that impression was more deeply confirmed. This was an organization that operated with a high degree of integrity and professionalism, and its members treated each other with exceptional regard and respect. Plus, they were having fun.

After my entertainment and speaking presentation, the CEO of the organization took the microphone to close the annual event. I've heard many such speeches from many leaders, and I was surprised by the content of his address.

He told three stories of things that had personally happened to him during the course of that year. Each represented a situation in which he had made a mistake—had failed to act on or had not lived up to his own hopes for excellence. There was no punch line, no big finish describing how he had redeemed himself or triumphed in the end by overcoming obstacles. What he communicated was the honest fabric of being human, of being up against the challenges of everyday life and the need for an even greater effort to reach excellence. His final words were simply, "I believe I can do better next year, and I invite you to do the same."

Such honest public testimony is rare. After experiencing the example of his personal integrity and complete lack of posturing, I no longer wondered how this group functioned so effectively. While the first rule is based on the fear that it's not okay to be ourselves, this leader communicated that excellence arises out of our authenticity.

Let us not forget that family systems are also organizations. They can flourish or flounder depending upon how embedded the rules are in our familial patterns. Chief among the rules that plague us in our families is the rule *be normal,* where we shame our children or even our partners into behaving like someone we wish them to be rather than supporting them to express themselves simply and uniquely. To instill freedom of expression in a child is to arm them for a lifetime with the ability to communicate.

Communication is vital to organizational success and requires our authenticity.

CHAPTER 1 SUMMARY

THE FIRST RULE WE WERE BORN TO BREAK IS:

Be Normal

THE FIRST MISBEHAVIOR IS:

Be Authentic

THE BENEFIT OF BREAKING THIS RULE IN A GROUP IS:

Communication

Excellence is an expression of differences. The first misbehavior, *be authentic*, is based on self-acceptance and knowing it's okay to be different. The idea that we should *be normal*, however, engenders shame in us and disconnects us from an experience of joy.

Defying Expectations

Any time we muster the courage to challenge normal patterns we're going to run into resistance from others who have an investment in those patterns. If we're able to ignore the opinions of the normal world as we move past cultural expectations, what we find on the other side is a whole new vista of possibilities and potential.

Doing What We Love

We are trained to hide our differences, not to stand out and openly live them. We are kept in line by the threat of being called a show-off, of being shunned or excluded, yet as we honor our passion consistently, such threats will recede into the distance, and no longer dissuade us from shining.

Being Spontaneous

Each of the seven rules invites us to forget who we really are and take part in a rule-script that disconnects us from our potential. When we try to pretend that we're like everyone else, we separate ourselves from the reality of the moment and the kind of spontaneity that can make our lives workable, rich, and fulfilling. If we can relax and remember the option of playfulness when a rule-script has been set in motion, we can often step outside of its influence.

Communication channels open when the members of any group take responsibility for expressing their experiences openly and authentically.

We would be well served to remember the words of Whoopi Goldberg, who reminds us, "Normal is just a cycle on the washing machine."

BE NORMAL
is the first rule we were born to break.

2

AVOID MISTAKES

It's interesting to consider that so much of comedy surrounds the imagery and circumstance of falling down. A man slipping and falling on a banana peel is the quintessential depiction of physical comedy. Why do we laugh when others fall down? Perhaps we realize the important role that mistakes play in the process of growth and discovery. In contrast to our culture's almost pathological desire to avoid any type of failure, we may find it delightful to reconnect to the power of error, accident and risk.

Many wonderful things in life, from inventions to relationships and from works of art to recipes, have been discovered by accident. Comedian Tony Follari points out that "a craftsman polishes his work, but a comedian polishes his errors." To engage in polishing our errors is a worthy description of excellence. But to polish mistakes we have to be willing to make them.

If you're not falling down every now and again, it's a sign you're not doing anything very innovative.

Woody Allen

As children, we are oriented to risk, experiment, and explore. As our survival becomes more assured, however, our exploration slows. Once we have explored and mastered our life circumstance to a reasonable extent, we turn our energies toward protecting ourselves from the sting of mistakes.

As adults, we turn toward the preservation of territory and property. This includes striving to protect and defend our knowledge. Included in what we consider knowledge are our perspectives, points of view, and ways of thinking about things. Once we've arrived at a set of beliefs about the way things are in the world, we tend to stick with them and are less inclined to question their accuracy or to seek out other perspectives.

Any pursuit of excellence, however, requires us to keep exploring and growing in both body and mind. Our cultural conditioning to play it safe and avoid all mistakes must be challenged.

☆

THE SECOND ACTION OF **INTELLIGENT MISBEHAVIOR** IS:

Take Chances

Crossing the Line

The first time I remember seeing a unicycle was on the floor of a Toys"R"Us store. I was completely captivated by the novelty of this circus prop and curious about what it would be like to ride it.

Responding to my fascination, my parents purchased it for me. I gradually learned to ride it while circling the ping-pong table in our family room and used the table to support myself as I traveled around its perimeter.

I can remember the frustration I felt in my initial efforts to ride this unique machine. It seemed impossible to me that one could ever learn to balance on a unicycle. The breakthrough I eventually had in the learning process occurred when it dawned on me that it *was* impossible. I finally understood that the only thing I could do on the unicycle was to allow myself to fall—to intentionally give up my balance and then chase that elusive balance point by pedaling toward it.

Metaphorically, this represents the process of moving toward excellence, which is always a balance between doing nothing at all and going too far. Before we can learn how much is just right in relationship to making efforts, we have to go too far and cross the line. It's only after we have fallen down a few times—or many—that we develop an exacting sense of how hard to lean toward our goals.

The process of unicycling is in fact nothing but the continuous act of falling and attempting to recover from the fall. If one does not "fall" on the cycle, it's impossible to move forward, since it is this seeming loss of balance that initiates any forward progression. Such is its nature. Anyone who is interested in growing toward excellence must seek a degree of imbalance to allow for forward progress. Our growth and progression is the activity of hovering at the point where we're just about to cross the line.

Once I had developed some proficiency at riding that first little unicycle, I took it out onto the streets of our neighborhood. I received a fair bit of attention and was satisfied with this for a few years. Then I learned that taller versions existed.

The next step was the order of a six-foot unicycle. The conflict between how badly I wanted to try riding it and the fear of falling was vivid in my experience the first time I sat on it. The consequences of taking a spill from this height were obviously more significant, but the principle was the same: lean first, fall forward, and ride as a result.

Years later, chance circumstances provided me with the opportunity to ride a unicycle that was twelve-feet tall. An acquaintance of our family had called to tell us about a boy she knew who was also a unicyclist. After he had developed some skill on a six-foot cycle like the one I had, his parents had supported him to order a custom-made twelve-foot unicycle that had recently been shipped to him from across the country.

So far, our friend reported, he hadn't been able to ride it. She wondered whether I might be able to help, and so a meeting was arranged.

I remember standing in the driveway of this boy's home when he brought the machine out of his garage and stood it up. He began describing how afraid he had become at the idea of getting on. He didn't know how to overcome his fear. I tried to encourage him with the excitement I experienced just from setting eyes on it. I asked him if he had tried riding it at all. He said that he'd only sat on it while holding onto a second-story window of his house.

We climbed a ladder to the roof of his garage, which was the only available way to mount the thing. I hoped he would actually push away from the house and give it a try. Once we were at the edge of the roof looking down, however, I understood completely what had stopped him. Instead of looking up at the seat of the cycle from the safety of the ground and thinking, I could do that, I was now looking at the distant pavement fifteen feet below and thinking, I could *die* doing that. This was no mere parlor trick. It was a serious undertaking.

After an hour of trying to get on it, the steam of any remaining enthusiasm gone, he said, "I just can't do it. You can try it." In truth I was now as scared as he was. A big part of me still wanted to, yet I was so frightened by the potential hazards of the stunt that I was shaking and distracted by all the excess adrenaline. I decided that my best option was to practice falling first so I'd know that when the moment came I could handle it. I pointed the towering machine toward my friend's front lawn instead of the pavement of the driveway, hopped up on the seat, and promptly pitched myself forward off balance and headed onto the grass before I had time to work myself into any more of a state about it.

My feet and legs stung from the impact, but the actual experience of falling prepared me to ride, whereas a purely imaginary fall had been messing with my head and preventing me from focusing. Our attempts to be certain that we won't make a mistake, fall, or err are often counterproductive to our aim. Sometimes intentionally crossing the line and making a mistake in a controlled setting helps diffuse the potential for our fear to distract us.

The plan worked. A few minutes later I was pedaling the unicycle down the driveway and out into the street, my head fifteen feet in the air, my eyes wide, and feeling on top of the world. I left his house that day the new owner of the machine and have used it for the finale of my performances ever since.

Our willingness to lose our balance and cross the line frees us to experience and explore our curiosity.

Trying New Things

One key to overcoming the rule of certainty is to pay attention to "what if" moments. "What if" moments are those instances when our curiosity prompts us to wonder what would happen if we took a new action in relationship to a known pattern or circumstance.

Early in my street performing career I heard about the infamous Venice Beach in California. Known once for its sublime natural beauty, its appeal today includes its history as a tourist attraction, a site for social experimentation, and a gathering spot for the celebrities, artists, and early beat poets of LA. It has been marked by phases of careful development as well as periods of such neglect that it became no more than a slum. For the past twenty years, Venice has sustained itself as a popular tourist destination and a congregation point for local athletes, movie stars, homeless people, and street entertainers.

My natural response to hearing about Venice Beach after having enjoyed substantial success as a street performer in Vancouver, British Columbia, for a number of years was to wonder what would happen if I performed there. So I made the trip to southern California by car, excited to apply my developed skills to the famous and popular US destination.

The day I arrived was a stellar, perfect sunny day in the City of Angels. Having found a place to park, I took my first walk down the Venice Boardwalk and observed early in the day a wide variety of street performers already fully engaged in the drawing and entertaining—and in some cases outright fleecing—of crowds.

The initial confidence that I felt in sharing my talent with Venice Beach admittedly waned in the seemingly lawless atmosphere of Venice itself. The place was crawling and seething with the sensational, and everything from sex to drugs to muscle was on display in the beautiful and the rich, the deranged and the destitute. I went back to my car to retrieve my props and equipment, anxious to squeeze into a performance spot before all the available spaces were taken.

I selected a spot on the Boardwalk between two other shows already in progress, each not more than seventy-five feet away.

My usual way of drawing a crowd for street shows involves the process of putting together my twelve-foot unicycle, which I travel with disassembled. Ordinarily, the spectacle of this shiny circus apparatus being prepared for performance is enough to get a core crowd to gather around and form the nucleus of an audience to build upon. In the environment of the already wildly sensational Venice Beach, however, this commanded almost zero interest.

After I had completed the assembly of my cycle, there were perhaps eight or ten people who had stopped and were waiting to see what would happen next, so I launched into my actual show, hoping the crowd would build. I pulled out all the stops. In peak physical condition at the time, I rolled out my best acrobatic stunts, juggling feats, and balancing amazements. What I needed was a solid foundation of spectators before turning to the finale of the show: mounting and riding the big unicycle.

It wasn't working.

I picked up a few extra onlookers over the course of fifteen minutes and lost just as many of my original few to the competing distractions of the locale. At that point, I looked toward the other performances and saw that to my left, not thirty feet away, was another performer who had set up next to me. It was then that I came to fully understand what I was up against. My competition was a dwarf who, with one arm completely missing and another that was no more than a stub, had rolled up on a skateboard, cordoned off a section of sidewalk with several traffic cones, scattered broken glass on the pavement, and begun break dancing on it.

I continued with my show, cutting out about half of my

material and making a beeline for the big finish of actually riding the unicycle. I made next to nothing in my hat. It was obvious that if I wanted to succeed in Venice, rather than balancing deftly on my tall unicycle I ought to have intentionally thrown myself from it onto the pavement, bleeding nonchalantly yet profusely, and then made a pitch for donations.

I could have viewed the experience of performing at Venice Beach as a complete failure and waste of a week of my time. Yet the dose of humility it provided deepened my character, strengthened my resolve to improve, and increased my gratitude for responsive audiences.

Another, potentially greater, mistake occurred on an occasion when I decided to experiment with an addition to the finale of my show, which typically involves lifting the watches of four volunteers whom I recruit to hold up my big unicycle and then enroll into a routine where it finally dawns on them that their watches are missing. Over the years I became quite adept at this slight and eventually wondered whether I could also learn to lift a volunteer's wallet. There was no way to satisfy that curiosity except to try.

My idea for how to make an entertaining routine out of this stunt was to lift a participant's wallet during my show and, without his knowledge, get his name, address, and birth date off his ID. Once I had this data, I would then pretend to be psychic and pull this information out of the air.

At the time, I was appearing at one of North America's premier resort sites performing outdoor shows in the village area to summer tourists. I had a very large crowd gathered by the end of the show in which I intended to introduce my brilliant addition to the act, and I was practically giddy that I had actually managed to lift the wallet of one of my volunteers, though it hadn't been easy.

I stood in front of the man I had just stolen it from. Facing the audience, I carefully pulled out the wallet with my back to him and shielded it from his view so I could let the crowd in on the trick as I gathered the information I needed to continue. As I flipped it open, the first thing both the crowd and I saw, glinting in the sunlight in its full glory, was a shiny gold detective's badge.

I had lifted the wallet of an undercover cop.

What followed may have been one of the only times in history that a pickpocket has nervously and frantically used his skills of stealth and misdirection to replace stolen property in due haste, rather than make off with it. My audience had a blast, and unless somebody from that crowd told him about it, the officer never knew.

In many cases, when we reach for something that turns out to be a mistake, we can make the necessary corrections and move on. Of course, our risks ought to intend a positive result, and what we're risking should be ours to risk, not someone else's money, reputation, or safety. There are many risks we can take that do not endanger others and where the worst thing that can happen is that we look a little silly, have to apologize, or clean up a bit of a mess.

The World's Funniest Waiter routine that is now one of the trademarks of my corporate meeting work also came about from a "what if" moment.

I had been hired to perform my physical comedy show onstage for a group of five hundred bankers. I arrived early to preset all of my props and then waited in the hallway of the banquet hall for lunch to be served before I would go on.

Suddenly the alarms and sprinklers went off in the kitchen, and the hallway filled with smoke. A fire that had started in the kitchen was quickly extinguished, but the entire lunch that was to be served to the hungry bankers was ruined. A plan was made to import food from another nearby hotel, but there would be a forty-five minute wait for the stomachs of the assembled executives. I understood where the term "bellyaching" came from as word got around among the ravenous crowd that lunch was on hold. The event producer who had hired me was panicking, fearing a massive walkout on her event.

Wanting to help fill the gap, I wondered what would happen if I put on a server's apron and headed out into the ballroom acting like an eccentric waiter as a way to entertain the guests. I assumed that people would know right away that my exaggerated character was a put-on, but the group took me very seriously and got hooked into the theater of it without suspecting it was a joke.

It was then that the possibilities for the routine dawned on me, and twenty years later the act is the cornerstone of my corporate work. The accident that day and my impulse to experiment with it ultimately provided one of the most distinct elements I offer as a meeting presenter.

To misbehave by *taking chances* means we can embrace our desire for new experiences, new relationships, and new ways of being.

Imagining Possibilities

In my senior year of high school I applied to a variety of schools and universities. Among the options I had seriously considered was the famous Ringling Brothers and Barnum and Bailey Clown College in Florida. The clown school served as the gateway for the training and instruction of clowns for the well-known Ringling Circus.

I told a close performer friend, Skip, who was also graduating from school that year, about the Ringling program. He expressed an interest, and since I had been accepted to Webster University by that time, I no longer had any use for my application to Clown College and I gave it to him.

Skip was accepted into the competitive program, eventually graduated, and then got offered a job with the circus.

Skip's willingness to apply to the Ringling school, his dedication to the training program, and his acceptance of an offer to clown for real with the Greatest Show on Earth were all demonstrations of overcoming the rule of certainty. Clown College was an untraditional choice for a high school graduate and promised little in its breadth of options for a future career or livelihood. Though plenty of people told this to Skip, he was undeterred. Circus life itself is hard and uncertain, and indeed when tragedy strikes it's the clowns who are called upon to help everyone cope, as the famous Stephen Sondheim song "Send in the Clowns" illustrates.

In April of 1980, the musical *Barnum* made its debut on the Broadway stage in New York City. The show was about the life of the infamous hoaxer and circus producer P. T. Barnum himself.

It logged 854 performances and won several Tony awards before eventually closing on Broadway and launching a national tour that played extended runs in some of the largest cities of North America.

As budding thespians in high school, Skip and I dreamed of performing one day in a Broadway show, as did our circle of theater friends. After graduating, we all went our separate ways: attending universities that were known for their theater programs, migrating to Los Angeles to court stardom in Hollywood, or moving to New York City to seek theatrical success.

Skip seemed to have taken the path that was least likely to result in a respectable career as an actor. One day, however, a Broadway casting rep visited the circus looking for skilled circus performers to cast in chorus roles for *Barnum*'s national tour. Skip's talent and enthusiasm stood out, and he was suddenly a member of the esteemed Actors' Equity union making a very good living as a bonafide actor and chorus member of a Broadway musical.

Now our story fast-forwards to the finish of the national tour a year later and the start of a second tour. National tours for Broadway shows are typically followed by a second tour called a "bus and truck" tour. They play in smaller cities and towns all across North America for shorter periods in less populated areas.

One day I got an excited and breathless phone call from Skip as he stood on a busy New York street corner at a pay phone. He was in Manhattan in the midst of rehearsals for the *Barnum* bus and truck tour which he had been invited to join. He said that he had overheard the director speaking about the show's need for a swing and that the director intended to hold a general audition for the part a few days later.

A "swing" is a particular kind of understudy who has no regular role but backs up many performers in a show. Swings are particularly crucial for bus and truck tours since the travel and performance schedules are grueling. The *Barnum* bus and truck tour was scheduled to play seventy cities in a nine-month period. As a tour such as this wears on, its cast wears down. Performers become tired, ill and injured, and a qualified replacement for everyone must be waiting in the wings. Thus the invention of the swing.

Skip was telling me that he had somehow persuaded the director to audition me alone prior to holding a cattle call for the rest of the professional acting community in all of New York City—talented performers who would happily queue up around the block for a shot at such a job.

The swing role for the *Barnum* tour was unique. While the swings would have to learn all the songs and lyrics, all the lines, every dance step and blocking cue for every musical number for every individual chorus member, they were also responsible for acquiring enough competencies in each circus discipline to perform that specialty in the show. I was to arrive in New York prepared to demonstrate as many of these skills as I could and to be auditioned for my abilities in acting, dancing, and singing.

Skip needed to know then and there if I were in so he could tell the director to wait to see me or move forward with general auditions. And there was a catch. Only a week of rehearsals remained prior to the start of the tour. If I got the part, I'd have to be prepared to stay.

The upshot of all this was that I had to wave goodbye to my

hometown and hang up my life as I currently knew it on the chance that a busy Broadway director across the country would find me suitable to the needs of his production. There on the phone, considering all this, my mind was spinning with questions, my body charged with mixed emotion. There was no question that fear was present as I contemplated the decision.

The desire to be certain of my future loomed in front of me as I considered what I had: a life that I enjoyed that was ordered, under my control, and offered a reasonable degree of predictability. I had momentum with my work as a local performer. I was becoming better known, and it had taken time to build that reputation and a clientele. Was I willing to risk it all for a chance at something that sounded intriguing and exciting but was in reality completely unknown?

The decision was only made when I imagined the possibilities that would open up if I took the risk and succeeded. It was an Actors' Equity job, which meant an equity card and access to equity auditions and the world of professional theater. In addition, it would be a chance to do what I loved while getting well paid and visiting many parts of the country where I had never been. I knew I would later regret not going for it if I didn't try out for the part.

Forty-eight hours and very little sleep later, I sat in my seat en route to JFK International Airport and tried to rest. My audition was scheduled to take place during the cast lunch break that very day at noon. My flight was due to arrive at 10:45 a.m. and I knew it was a thirty-minute cab ride from the airport to the studio in Manhattan, an hour at the most if traffic was bad.

Everything was looking good until I woke with a bit of a start as our plane bounced across the top of some nasty clouds just outside of New York City and the seat belt sign went on. I had dozed off, and now it was 10:30 a.m. as we descended toward JFK airport. The bumps got worse while we cut through banks of grim-looking thunderheads. Suddenly, the plane pulled up its nose and we started climbing again. The copilot explained that a volatile storm system had blown in and it was too risky to attempt a landing. We were going to have to circle and wait for conditions to improve before making another approach.

Helplessly, I sat and watched out the window. We circled—and circled. Twenty minutes, a half hour, forty minutes passed, and we were still circling. The doorway to my potential future was now all but closed. The chances of landing, deplaning, and getting to the theater on time were virtually nonexistent.

My taxi pulled up in front of the studio at 12:55 p.m. I ran into the building and up to the rehearsal loft. "Where have you been?" Skip asked. "We're starting rehearsal in a few minutes. You missed the audition." I took a seat in a set of bleachers off to one side of the large rehearsal space. Skip ran off to tell the director that I had arrived and see what he wanted to do. Oddly, my thoughts were not focused on the worry that the director might not see me or that I was essentially alone in New York City without a job or a home, no return flight, and no particular direction or plan. I mostly remember feeling excited and interested in what would happen next.

Skip ran back to where I was sitting and told me the director wanted me to wait, that he would see me at the end of the day.

I watched the rehearsal and waited in a kind of altered state of heightened awareness, fully present. I had accepted the uncertainty of the situation and my attention was focused on the possibilities.

When the audition time finally arrived, I was sharp and clear. After a twenty-minute audition I was given the job on the spot.

The next nine months were nothing but a training ground for developing an even deeper relationship to accepting uncertainty. My job as a swing threw me constantly into situations where I had to improvise and leap—sometimes literally—into situations that were unknown and challenging.

A whole life opened up that has served me immeasurably in both my performing career and in my personal life. It was a revelation to experience the freedom I actually had to move forward in situations even when I had doubts and was unsure. The freedom I found came from putting my attention on the possibility of positive outcomes.

Innovation

The rule that says we must avoid mistakes in an organizational setting can shut down the potential for growth and effective problem solving. Innovative responses to challenges flourish in corporate cultures that value curiosity, exhibit a love of learning, and encourage risk taking and trying things without knowing if they will work. Obviously there are aspects of many industries where taking chances is inappropriate, especially where the physical safety of oneself and others is at stake. Yet there are always areas in every organization where a willingness to try something new can result in dramatic organizational improvements.

I once performed at the Sheraton Sand Key Resort in Tampa

Bay, Florida, for a company that wanted to have a beach-party-theme function that involved actually having the party on the beach.

A tent was set up about thirty feet from the high-tide surf line. Cables from the hotel, about a quarter mile away, were run across the wide white-sand beach down to the tent. Decorated with nautically themed fabric and patterns, the tent was lit on the inside by the soft glow of low-hanging lamps and was gently serenaded by the sound of cresting waves. It was evident that someone had put intention and effort into creating a meeting environment that was unique, refreshing, and delightful. The feel was entirely magical.

I can tell you from many years of experience and countless numbers of events that this is far from the usual case. If you're a professional who regularly attends meetings, I'm sure you agree. Noticeably absent at many events is the willingness of planners to try anything new.

A stage had been set up at one end of the tent for my show, and after completing the waiter routine I began the stage portion of my presentation. The audience was enthralled and responsive, and the show proceeded without a hitch—until an unsuspecting dune buggy driver ran over the power cord in the sand and the entire tent was plunged into a blackout on a moonless night.

The timing couldn't have been worse. I was on top of my twelve-foot unicycle in the middle of the finale of my show. I idled back and forth in the dark in a panic, trying to orient myself on top of the unicycle without the visual reference points crucial to balance. Not only was I elevated on the unicycle, I was on top of a stage that was already three feet off the ground.

As my eyes quickly began to adjust, I noticed that the only source of illumination was the individual points of light from tiny tea candles that had been set out on all the table rounds.

Within several seconds of the blackout, one gentleman picked up one of the tea candles from his table and began walking toward the stage, organizing others on the way to move forward with their candles as well. Within half a minute, the audience of three to four hundred people was completely surrounding the stage, holding their candles high. Collectively, they shed ample light on the surrounding area to allow me to safely dismount.

I believe the effort that had been made to create an original venue provided an atmosphere for fresh and open thinking among these guests. The idea to bring the candles to the stage was sparked by an environment of experimentation and the willingness to try something different and new.

Innovation increases when any organization intentionally addresses the second rule: *avoid mistakes.*

CHAPTER 2 SUMMARY

THE SECOND RULE WE WERE BORN TO BREAK IS:

Avoid Mistakes

THE SECOND MISBEHAVIOR IS:

Take Chances

THE BENEFIT OF BREAKING THIS RULE IN A GROUP IS:

Innovation

We discover what is possible by risking. The courage to *take chances* can lead us forward toward learning and discovery. The concept that all action we take should be accompanied by certainty, however, causes us to wallow in hesitation and fear.

Crossing the Line

Our attempts to be certain that we won't make a mistake, fall, or err are often counterproductive to our aim. Sometimes intentionally crossing the line and making a mistake in a controlled setting helps diffuse the potential for our fear to distract us.

Trying New Things

Curiosity is an enormously powerful force. Working in tandem with other feelings of excellence, it moves us in the direction of growth. With curiosity we are compelled to discover new experiences and new ways of doing things. There are reasonable fears and we ought to pay attention to them. Compared to the fears we indulge on a daily basis, however, they are few.

Imagining Possibilities

We have opportunities every day to imagine ideal outcomes and empower them through visualization and intention. Perhaps there is something we've always wanted to learn but we doubt our ability, or we've shied away from speaking to someone we'd like to meet because we're afraid of rejection, or we have an idea for our own business, yet doubt we can be successful. When we allow ourselves to imagine the possibilities that wait for us on the other side of risk, we can put our hesitations and fear in perspective and free ourselves to act.

The rule that says we must avoid mistakes has at its root the desire to avoid what we have been conditioned to view as failures. The more we equate any kind of mistake with the broader notion of failure, the more we block the exploratory process on which excellence is based. Within the context of excellence, the only failure is to refuse to take the risks that are an integral part of the learning and growing process. We can orient ourselves to intelligent risks, but life never ceases to be a risky venture. As Helen Keller reminded us, "Life is either a daring adventure, or nothing."

Innovative responses to challenges flourish in corporate cultures that value curiosity, exhibit a love of learning, and encourage taking risks and trying things without knowing if they will work.

AVOID MISTAKES
is the second rule we were born to break.

BE INDEPENDENT

WHO WE ARE AS INDIVIDUALS BLOSSOMS as we discover and learn who we are *in relationship to our world*. We do this by deeply connecting with it, not by withdrawing from it. A mature individual is able to draw support and strength from others and provide a distinct contribution to the world. Our individuality suffers when we cut ourselves off from an exchange of help by trying to remain wholly independent. We often isolate ourselves by appearing to be self-sufficient. We fortify our walls of in-dependence when we turn increasingly to technology for infor-mation and entertainment rather than investing in the challenges and rewards of human relationship.

Our tendency is to regard vulnerability as a weakness rather than seeing it as an inherent strength. We treat vulnerability as something we ought to grow out of as soon as possible, when in actuality it is essential to our excellence.

Children, as an example, are never too proud to receive help and support. Their vulnerability is an intelligent response to the truth of their circumstance, since they are clearly dependent upon their environment. Their innocence and a lack of defense bring them immediate support. Any adult who has ever heard the plaintive cry of a child in a supermarket who has been separated from his or her mother knows the power of this vulnerability.

> *I went to a bookstore and asked the saleswoman, "Where's the self-help section?" She said if she told me, it would defeat the purpose.*
>
> George Carlin

A recognition that we cannot succeed on our own is a central component of excellence. Adults who can ask for help are able to grow and succeed through the power of their vulnerability. Adults who have forgotten this not only suffer as a result themselves, they also pass on the disease of independence to their kids, mostly through modeling—sometimes with the literal words, "Don't bother me."

In this way we are trained to watch out for ourselves and avoid relying upon anyone else for support. Oriented to the rule *be independent*, we buffer ourselves from the experience of trust, an essential factor in excellence, especially for endeavors that are team related.

☆

THE THIRD ACTION OF **INTELLIGENT MISBEHAVIOR** IS:

Ask for Help

Asking with Passion

I was ten years old when my father took me to the Milwaukee Civic Center one evening for a "surprise." I had no idea what we were about to see, but I knew it had to be something special enough to warrant the temporary suspension of bedtime on a school night.

We took our seats in the balcony section of the theater. They were royal red. The curtain was red, too—plush velvet with yellow tassels across the bottom. Everything about it indicated that something grand was about to appear on that stage. I waited excitedly for what would occur. The curtain finally went up, and there onstage was…nothing, just an empty stage. And with the exception of the body of just one individual, that stage would remain completely empty that night, yet I would leave flooded with inspiration.

The performance was by Marcel Marceau, universally acclaimed as the world's greatest mime. As a ten-year-old I wasn't sure what I had just seen. I only knew that it had communicated something fascinating about the power of the human imagination and that it was a rare demonstration of excellence.

I vividly recall having a mime troupe visit our school shortly thereafter. Wanting to learn everything I could about the art, I was riveted to the troupe's performance. I don't think I blinked the entire time.

Halfway through their show, the members mimed that they wanted a volunteer from the audience. There were four hundred kids in the school gym that day, and half of us raised our hands, but no one raised their hand the way I did. I stood up and stretched my hand so high that the tips of my toes were barely touching the floor. My whole body was asking, begging for the chance to be on stage with them.

This is clearly a very vulnerable position—to ask so openly for what we need—because there is the danger that we'll be rejected. And, in fact, sometimes we will be rejected when we extend ourselves this way. Yet, unquestionably, when we are willing to be vulnerable enough to communicate our needs, our odds of being helped, given opportunities, and being supported are immeasurably improved over not asking at all.

Those of us who ask, and ask with passion, enjoy far greater success in getting what we want and need than those who don't. So get on the tips of your toes, stretch your hand high, and sport an "Ooo! Ooo! Pick Me!" attitude.

And yes, they picked me.

Committing Before Asking

As I mentioned earlier, I spent many years working and traveling as a street performer before I became more involved with providing corporate presentations.

After a number of years doing street shows in my adopted hometown of Vancouver, I wanted to try working internationally. From the time I was very young I had dreamed of becoming a traveling troubadour, wandering freely between towns and living off of what I could make by busking.

Busking is the activity of offering unticketed performances in public places and then passing a hat for donations at the conclusion of the show. It is a unique form of business where a product is offered without charge, enjoyed by the recipient, and then the consumer is given the freedom to offer payment in return if the product is perceived as being valuable.

This principle is generally understood in the business world as being the key to building strong customer relations. Provide value and the customers will follow.

My busking and traveling dream came true one year at the conclusion of a North American summer as it dawned on me that the approaching fall and winter on our continent meant the onset of spring/summer on the other side of the planet.

I had heard about busking "pitches" (performing areas where busking is legal and potentially profitable) in both New Zealand and Australia. It didn't take much convincing to enroll my girlfriend at the time into the adventure. To top it off, we planned to do the trip by bicycle, carrying both camping equipment and a twelve-foot unicycle I had specially designed for the trip in a trailer that I towed behind my road bike.

It was an incredible journey through a beautiful and rugged land, spiced by the challenge of supporting ourselves through performances that we offered in everything from campgrounds to small resorts to public markets that we came across along the way. The positive response we received was exponentially increased by the vulnerability of our situation, putting ourselves out to audiences across the globe without any backup plan or safety net.

We found ourselves in the city of Hamilton, New Zealand, at Christmas time that year. I was performing at a local market doing shows for small crowds, and we were squeaking by, making just enough money to live on. Every day was a workday, and we found ourselves knocking out shows on Christmas Eve at the marketplace.

Just before the market closed, we were packing up equipment and preparing to cycle onward to the next town. We didn't know where we would stay that night or what we would do to celebrate. Walking by the kiosk of a toymaker, we stopped to appreciate his handmade toys, and in chatting with him we began sharing some of the details of our wandering exploits. Before we knew it the man was out from behind his table and giving us directions on how to get to his home, adamantly insisting that we spend that evening and Christmas day with him and his family.

We gratefully accepted, and it turned into one of the most memorable holidays of my lifetime. The true spirit of generosity and giving could not have been more vividly demonstrated as we were hosted in a quaint Kiwi family home in rural Hamilton, treated to delicious home-cooked food, and surrounded by the warmth of an extended family. To have a set of complete strangers welcome us so openly and with such hospitality gave the spirit of Christmas profound meaning.

When we live with commitment to our calling and engage the vulnerability of providing value first, our life itself becomes a form of asking that generates a response before we have even made a formal request.

Being Honest and Direct

Street performance is really my first love as a presentation venue. I've continued to busk at some festivals and at the Granville Island Public Market in Vancouver, BC, even as I've gotten busier with corporate presentations. The challenges it provides are an unmatched form of performing practice, and it affords an excellent opportunity to experiment with new material. The money can be worthwhile as well during the busier times of year when the crowds are larger.

One perfect summer day at Granville Island I was looking forward to a couple of shows I had been scheduled for on one of the most lucrative stages. Following my first show I spoke with a woman who jokingly asked me if I wanted to donate the money I had just made to help her replace the hot water heater that had unexpectedly burst and flooded her basement while she was on vacation. As she walked away, the joke began to turn into a serious idea that I decided to experiment with during my second performance.

I did my usual show, but after collecting donations at the end, I announced to the audience that I was going to give someone in the crowd a chance to win all the money I had just received.

I said that anyone could win the money. All they had to do was come up in front of the crowd and give a thirty-second speech on behalf of their plan or dream and describe how they would use the cash. Then the audience members themselves would vote for the most worthy recipient.

At least one hundred hands instantly shot into the air, so I selected twenty people at random and invited them up to the stage. They stood in a long line: men, women and children.

I started at one end and handed the microphone to a little boy who shouted out, "I think I should get the money, because if you gave it to me I could get a lot of candy!" Everyone laughed, and I felt the delight of having tried a new idea, anticipating all the fun that was about to come from these twenty volunteers contesting for the cash.

But then something unexpected happened.

One by one the microphone was passed along, and instead of being more entertained, the crowd grew more and more silent as each individual, some of them extremely nervous about being in front of an audience, took the risk of speaking about their cause—charities they volunteered for, organizations they believed in. Passionate petitions were made for the homeless, the hungry, single mothers, and nonprofits with real vision. The further down the line we moved, the more each person brought to his or her appeal.

Finally we came to the last participant, a blue-collar worker in overalls with unkempt hair. It has been noted that the fear of speaking in public routinely ranks higher than the fear of death. The look on this man's face showed it. He had perhaps never spoken in public before in his life, yet something had motivated him to take a place on stage and attempt to convince a large gathering of strangers why he ought to get all the money that waited in my hat.

Taking the microphone, he quietly began telling us about his grown son, who months earlier had suffered a severe injury. Out of work for months, trying to get by, his son was just several hundred dollars short of the money he needed for an operation that would get him back to work. This distraught and troubled father spoke not just for his son, but for the needs of his daughter-in-law and grandchildren.

This man's cause was not any greater than that of the other people on stage, but with his shaking knees and trembling voice, it was clear that no one else who spoke that day risked themselves with more vulnerability than he did.

The audience unanimously rewarded his courage, his love, and his simplicity by voting him the deserving recipient of their donations. Beneath the touching display of his appeal was a proud, hardworking man who overcame his own deeply engrained habit of remaining independent by honestly and directly asking for help.

Teamwork

The rule *be independent* is a serious hindrance to group success within organizations. Teamwork is a result of vulnerability, trust, and the understanding that to succeed in the absence of help from others is impossible.

As I mentioned earlier, my job as a swing on the *Barnum* tour was an unpredictable one. Being a full-time understudy, my duty involved sitting backstage and waiting. Periodically, the stage manager would arrive breathless in our dressing room, where I might be sitting with a book, and announce that I was on because one of the performers was late to the theater, had twisted an ankle on stage, or wasn't feeling well. Since there were sixteen unique roles that I understudied, it was difficult at the beginning to remember all the distinct parts. Most of the time I would throw on the appropriate costume and run out into the middle of a complex production number in some degree of confusion. It was a challenge to remember who I was supposed to be, what I was supposed to sing, what dance step I needed to do, what I might need to catch or balance, or who I might have to sidestep before they landed on me from some circus apparatus above.

I learned to pay attention in the moment and trust my cast members. I was completely dependent upon getting help from them. They would find ways to whisper or gesture where I ought to be and what I ought to be doing. They'd get me into the right place at the right time if I remained attentive to them and open to their help. I would follow their lead and just smile as the scenes and production numbers unfolded, as if I knew exactly what I was doing. The audience couldn't tell the difference. It was a true team effort.

Months later in the tour, after I finally had it all down, I felt a twinge of longing for the sense of camaraderie and connection that came from needing my fellow actors' help. They found other ways to keep things interesting for me, like hiding props, changing small cue lines, and modifying choreography without warning. While my team members made things workable for me when it was more than I could handle, they also kept me working hard, necessitating that I remain sharp and alert after the usual routines ceased to challenge my growth and capacity.

Teamwork is, of course, an essential component of organizational success.

CHAPTER 3 SUMMARY

THE THIRD RULE WE WERE BORN TO BREAK IS:

Be Independent

THE THIRD MISBEHAVIOR IS:

Ask for Help

THE BENEFIT OF BREAKING THIS RULE IN A GROUP IS:

Teamwork

The third misbehavior, *ask for help*, is based on the understanding that vulnerability is a strength, not a weakness. The expectation that we should be able to do everything ourselves, however, teaches us to cut ourselves off from support and separates us from the experience of trust.

Asking with Passion

Those of us who ask, and ask with passion, enjoy far greater success in getting what we want and need than those who don't. Yet we're trained to hold back, take care of ourselves, and avoid having to rely on or trust anyone else to help us get what we want. We approach excellence when we realize, despite our cultural training, that nothing can stop us from getting on the tips of our toes, stretching our hand high, and sporting an "Ooo! Ooo! Pick Me!" attitude.

Committing Before Asking

When we live with commitment to our calling and engage the vulnerability of providing value first, our life itself then becomes a form of asking that generates a response before we've even made a formal request for help. Others are naturally moved to help us when we surrender ourselves to our true purpose. Such an orientation always attracts support.

Being Honest and Direct

Openness and innocence are powerful catalysts for generating support. Being honest and direct in our asking communicates our vulnerability, and others respond. Whining, complaining, overdramatizing, pleading, whimpering, guilt-tripping, blaming, justifying, and acting like a victim do not qualify as forms of vulnerability. Excellence requires that we stop exercising these methods of trying to meet our needs and confront the reality of our vulnerability in life.

Ultimately, we are the ones who determine whether we live in isolation and withdrawal, perhaps bitter that no one will come to our aid, or enjoy the many sources of help that are waiting for us once we've become vulnerable enough to receive them.

Teamwork occurs within a group when its members experience the limitations of independence and admit that help from others is necessary for success.

BE INDEPENDENT
is the third rule we were born to break.

☆

STAY COMFORTABLE

A COMPONENT OF MATURITY, and certainly of excellence, is the ability to connect to the quality of diligence that children naturally possess. Their focused and engaged play eventually becomes a love for work. Our eventual ability to delay immediate gratification as adults comes from having learned to enjoy the process of making efforts when we're young.

As we are introduced in our formative years to the conveniences and luxuries of modern life, however, we become disconnected from the natural instincts that drive our growth and a healthy orientation to determination. Never have we been so free to purchase pleasures and to avoid any version of discomfort. We are trained to believe this should make us happy, yet the real result of our orientation to quick-pleasure fixes is that we cannot achieve any form of growth that requires even a minor sacrifice for its success.

> *The trouble with jogging is that the ice falls out of your glass.*
>
> MARTIN MULL

In a spiral of disconnection from our natural inclination toward work, we require more distractions to escape the feeling of depression. We turn to the panacea of comfort, and the cycle intensifies.

☆

THE FOURTH ACTION OF **INTELLIGENT MISBEHAVIOR** IS:

Be Determined

Not Quitting

When my son Nate was just an infant, we would often carry him around the house in a backpack carrier. I remember one day needing to wash by hand a large stack of dishes and putting him on my back so he could be near me while I worked. He liked movement and activity in general so was ordinarily very happy in the carrier. This day was no different. As I was bending forward, straightening up, and swinging left and right in the process of washing, he made no sounds, which meant that he was content. The only real indication of his presence was that he was engrossed in tracing imaginary lines on my back, shoulders, and head with his finger. I was happy that he was happy, and we got the dishes done.

When I took off the backpack with him in it, he looked radiant and delighted. Then I noticed he was holding something in both hands. I quizzically looked at one of his hands to figure out what he was clutching and, prying his fingers back, saw that it was the cap from a laundry marker, the kind we used in the kitchen and kept in a jar above the sink.

At that point, I got a sinking feeling, and confirmed the bad news as I looked at his other hand and saw the weapon he was happily wielding. He had, as a matter of fact, not been tracing on the back of the backpack, my shirt, my neck and head with his little finger, but with black permanent marker.

Children will diligently pursue unfamiliar objects and phenomena within their grasp or line of vision with more necessity than they will seek rest or relaxation. To adults, of course, this just looks like play. It serves us, however, to recognize the value of such continuous participation in life.

The international community of street performers possesses an admirable work ethic. As I've already mentioned, the basis of the transaction between a performer and a customer involves the delivery of an entertainment product for free. An audience member provides compensation in return only if he or she perceives that something of value has been offered.

No written code or bylaws exist to govern the behavior of street performers. This is largely unnecessary since the way they're paid creates a self-regulating system for the quality control of entertainers. When a performer demonstrates a respect for his or her customers and delivers a product with integrity and professionalism, those customers tend to respond favorably with their donations. Entertainers who don't want to work hard on behalf of their audiences do not thrive or often even survive in the industry.

From the first step into an empty space in which a crowd of strangers must somehow be gathered, and in the absence of any guarantee of a favorable result, street performing is anything but a comfortable experience.

One of the unwritten codes that street performers share is that you give each and every performance your all, and never bail. Bailing is when a performer begins a show and if it's not going well they quit, either because they're having a bad day, the crowd is unenthusiastic, or the audience is too small to make the kind of money that was hoped for.

I have been performing street shows for the Granville Island Public Market in Vancouver at the annual Canada Day celebration for many years. The weather factor is a significant one for street performers. When the skies are clear and temperatures are fair, it's heavenly. When it's pouring or freezing, it's disappointing, but one can stay home and sleep or rest, since it's clear there is no possibility of work. The worst circumstance for an entertainer is when conditions vacillate between promising skies and inclement weather. In this situation, a performer may start a show, spend forty-five minutes bringing the crowd to a peak of entertainment satisfaction, and then lose the audience as they run for cover before donations can be collected.

On one Canada Day my shows were ending like this as I tried to squeeze scheduled performances in between bouts of rain and thunderstorms. The time for what was designated to be my last show of the day arrived under the same skies that had already scattered two of the large crowds I had worked so hard to build, and I was feeling depressed about it. I was already imagining where I would go for dinner and what kind of beer I'd use to medicate my disappointment that the best busking day of the entire year had been a washout.

This is a standard feature of our susceptibility to the rule of comfort. The weight of a depressive or despondent mood calls out for us to relieve it with the distraction of comfort. Once our thoughts are enrolled into the pursuit of relief and we've begun to imagine the specifics of our escape, whether it's ice cream, a trip to the movies, or just a flop on the couch, it's a significant challenge to keep participating in the midst of an uncomfortable situation.

Standing on the performance area a few minutes before my time slot, I stared up at the dark clouds I was sure were taunting me. It had temporarily stopped raining, but I felt like Charlie Brown before Lucy and her football as she promised that she wouldn't pull it away again. I decided I just wasn't going to participate this time and started to pack up my equipment.

Then arrived my friend Owen Lean, a self-effacing and talented magician who performs a show of close-up magic on the street. He had been traveling internationally and had just arrived in Vancouver in time for Canada Day.

Owen asked what I was doing. When I indicated that I was

going home, he reminded me what our business is all about with an animated zeal. He waved the smelling salts of busking passion under my nose and basically called me on taking the easy way out of the day—telling me that he wanted to see me work—and provided personally to me what a good busker delivers to an audience: an infectious mood of possibility and enthusiasm for participating.

With my priorities properly reestablished, and convinced of the need to follow through, I was grateful for the encouragement from my colleague. And so I set up for the show.

It did in fact rain during my performance, sprinkling off and on, but I challenged my audience to stay with me, telling them I wouldn't quit on them if they didn't quit on me. Most of them remained with me through to the end. The money was not exceptional, but the experience was irreplaceable, as is any circumstance that reawakens our vision for excellence in the face of the rules.

Owen was up after me. I started him off by tossing a first bill into his hat and stayed to watch his show and support him in return.

It wasn't until later that day at home that I had a chance to sort the cash from the show. It is one of the greatest pleasures of street performing—slowly unfolding bills, stacking and counting coins, and registering the satisfaction that one has provided to a crowd of strangers who have voluntarily expressed their appreciation for one's efforts.

Once again I felt gratitude for my colleague who had kept me honest. No matter what our modern world manages to make comfortable for us, it will never be possible to realize excellence without developing habits of discipline.

Nearing the bottom of my hat, I took out an American one-dollar bill that had been folded over several times and slowly opened it flat to add to my stack. I stopped and stared for a moment before it registered that someone had tucked a one-hundred-dollar bill inside the one-dollar note. They had evidently been moved enough by my effort in the rain to silently and anonymously let me know that determination is still appreciated in this world.

Getting Obsessed

I was in my midtwenties when I attended my first International Jugglers' Association convention. It was 1983, in Purchase, New York. The central draw to the convention is the main hall, where jugglers from all over the world gather to share tricks, engage in passing, and watch each other practice. It's jugglers' heaven.

There were between four- and five-hundred jugglers in the gym that day when an inconspicuous ten-year-old walked in with his prop bag, set it down, and dumped out its contents to practice. As he began to work, both amateur and professional jugglers, some of the most accomplished in the world, one by one stopped what they were doing to watch this young boy matter-of-factly practice things they had not thought possible, especially for a boy of ten. Transfixed, we all slowly dropped to our knees to crouch or sit on the floor until the entire hall was silent, watching the boy named Anthony Gatto practice.

Having worked professionally as a vaudeville entertainer, Anthony's father, Nick Gatto, recognized the quality of diligence in his son and encouraged it. The sparks of that diligence were fanned into flames of obsession as the young Nick became entirely focused on the mastery of numerous tricks. His natural ability, when combined with proper coaching, resulted in indisputable excellence.

Today, at the age of thirty-seven, Anthony Gatto shows no signs of slowing down. He performs all over the world and has been setting world records in juggling since he was a teenager, holding eleven of them as of this writing, some having already stood for over a decade. Mark Calton, who is the head coach for the famous Cirque du Soleil touring division, remarks of Anthony, "I wish we could take your practice and work ethic and bottle it."

The result of being connected to diligence is that the individual naturally surpasses a standard threshold of discomfort and develops stamina—physically, emotionally, and mentally—in relationship to his or her life participation. That stamina leads to a feeling of vitality.

If we're lucky, such vitality can take on a life of its own and we enter into an escalating cycle of passion for achievement. The word "obsession" has a negative connotation, but those who have healthy obsessions experience an intensity of fulfillment that normal folks do not come to know. What looks from the outside like a lot of work is felt on the inside as great satisfaction.

Assuming No Limits

As a presenter and communicator of excellence in the corporate world, I can appreciate as well as anyone when a powerful message is publicly demonstrated.

One of my most memorable experiences of such an occurrence was at an event held by a large and well-known publishing company. It was a year-end party for their Careers group, which had just posted record-breaking sales numbers in an economy rife with underachieving sales divisions for most industries on the planet. Why such success? There are no doubt many reasons, but from my own perspective, the management of this particular division had an unusually evolved understanding of the components of excellence, particularly concerning the qualities of diligence and commitment.

The president of this Career Education group had some years ago given the job of his executive assistant to an intelligent and highly capable employee who had no university degree. In the process of marrying and raising a family, her formal educational path had taken a backseat to the realities of parenting and the practical need to work. Her boss's condition for offering the post, however, was that this woman continue to work at her own rate and speed toward obtaining her degree by correspondence while she was employed there. Years later, she did in fact complete her studies and graduated from a university in the state of Illinois, receiving her diploma through an online program.

I had been hired to perform my show, and as I was waiting at the back of the room for my slot in their evening event, the president took to the stage to bestow various awards upon many members of his staff. One of the awards, he explained, was a surprise. He then welcomed to the stage the president of the very university from which his assistant had received her diploma.

The president had flown the dignitary from Illinois to the site of this event in New Orleans to personally conduct a formal graduation ceremony, in full commencement attire, for his employee.

Though his assistant had been invited to attend the university's standard graduation, she had been unable to do so, given her practical commitments to her work and her family. Stunned by this honoring of her accomplishment, she walked slowly to the stage. Conspiring coworkers magically produced cap and gown, dressing her in them as she went forward to officially receive her diploma in front of her colleagues.

This was one of the most moving moments I have experienced in my years of working with hundreds of corporate entities. Given my love for my own livelihood and for being self-employed, it is extremely rare that I feel any degree of vocational attraction to even the most successful of companies, but the environment of excellence palpable in this organization had me fantasizing for a moment about how wonderful it would be to work for them.

It's easy to forget the necessity of challenging our limits and the joy of work—of learning, growing, and evolving. We often swap the fulfillment we can experience from hard work for the hope of perpetual comfort. On this day, we all rose to our feet in a standing ovation, honoring not just an individual but also the value of hard work—of going the extra mile and committing to growth, education, and excellence beyond the limits that we imagine for ourselves.

Productivity

The rule of comfort must be clearly addressed in our personal lives and then again in our organizations for productivity to be dramatically improved. Productivity in an organization results when determination is activated and encouraged in the group.

The Vancouver-based street performer program that I have mentioned several times is a prime example of productivity. For the past thirty years, rain or shine, the informal association of street performers who call Vancouver home has provided virtually nonstop entertainment for the locals and tourists who visit Granville Island. These performers have provided more shows and more hours of entertainment, music and culture than any professional theater in town, and it's not because they're paid well. It's because they are willing to break the rule of comfort, and this in turn keeps them deeply connected to their diligence and vitality in the work environment.

As an offering to the general public, I can hardly imagine a more productive endeavor. The rule of comfort is based on the lie that we can become fulfilled passively. We forget that the process of living and evolving is not meant to be comfortable, and we have been quietly lulled into cul-de-sacs of virtual existence where children no longer play in the street, we don't mow our own grass, and neighbors seldom cross paths.

The street performers I work with offer the equivalent of a public service message that reflects an observation made by the comedian Jason Love: "Life is what happens when you're not watching television."

Perhaps we feel this to be an unfair example, wondering how a determination that borders on obsession could apply to our average, everyday, uninteresting professions. Every entertainer who has ever drawn a crowd has faced the same dilemma. How do I make my job of standing in front of people as they walk past interesting and rewarding, for them and for me?

Whether we make coffee, deliver newspapers, sweep floors, crunch spreadsheet numbers, run corporations, or street perform, nothing interesting happens until we become committed to our position. We must apply ourselves with the full force of our determination to make our jobs engaging and rewarding, regardless of what they are. *Not quitting, getting obsessed,* and *assuming no limits* is a great place to start.

Productivity is a core issue for any organization, and it grows in direct proportion to how consistently we challenge the rule of comfort with determination.

CHAPTER 4 SUMMARY

THE FOURTH RULE WE WERE BORN TO BREAK IS:

Stay Comfortable

THE FOURTH MISBEHAVIOR IS:

Be Determined

THE BENEFIT OF BREAKING THIS RULE IN A GROUP IS:

Productivity

The fourth misbehavior, *be determined*, can protect us from the rule of comfort that convinces us that discomfort is a reason to quit. Without the active presence of determination in our lives we can become prone to depression.

Not Quitting

Conditioned into trying to stay comfortable, we become disconnected from the habit of making efforts and less tolerant of activities that call for us to persevere. Once our thoughts turn to the pursuit of relief and we've begun to imagine the specifics of our escape, whether it's ice cream, a trip to the movies, or just a flop on the couch, it's a significant challenge to keep participating in an uncomfortable situation. Commitment, follow-through, and the ability to grit it out through challenging or uncomfortable circumstances is a tremendously useful habit that we can only build one day at a time through practice.

Getting Obsessed

The downward decline that is set in motion when we become hypnotized by the rule of comfort eventually results in stagnation, not excellence. The notion of being obsessed with something has negative connotations for most of us, but there are healthy obsessions as well as unhealthy ones. The healthy ones may be exactly what we need to counter some of the ways in which we get stuck in our lives. Determination when fully blossomed takes the form of productive obsession.

Assuming No Limits

We have, unfortunately, forgotten the necessity of challenging our limits and the joy of work—of learning, growing, and evolving. We have replaced the fulfillment we can experience when we remember there is no top end to what we can achieve with a hope for perpetual comfort. The practice of assuming no limits requires that we surround ourselves with reminders of our potential and with other people who have an ardent and sincere wish to grow. Without active effort to keep ourselves inspired, we're likely to start arguing for our limitations rather than exceeding them.

Productivity in an organization results when determination is activated and encouraged in the group.

STAY COMFORTABLE
is the fourth rule we were born to break.

PRETEND YOU DON'T MATTER

As we come to realize how big and complex our world is, a feeling of being overwhelmed and powerless can overtake us. We might feel that our individual efforts don't matter. A sense of insignificance can cause us to stop believing we can make a difference. In feeling irrelevant, we lose our incentive to be present in our lives.

We have all but mastered a perpetually casual attitude as we take violence, the misfortune of others, the slow theft of our liberties and freedoms, the obesity rate of our population, and the poisoning of our environment in stride. The casualness of our culture, while we equate it with how relaxed, easygoing, and even free we are as a nation, is the barometer of our rejection of our personal significance.

The only thing wrong with doing nothing is that you never know when you're finished.

Anonymous

We have stopped believing that we matter, and when we cease to matter to ourselves, then little matters in our world. Eventually, the phrase "It Doesn't Matter" may become the more appropriate motto for U.S. currency than the words "In God We Trust."

Our excellence is dependent upon a powerful reconnection to our significance by exercising presence and recognizing that the smallest of our activities impacts our environment and others in ways we often cannot foretell.

When we have fallen prey to this fifth rule, we convince ourselves that the details of life are inconsequential, and we often ignore what is right in front of us and give ourselves permission to tune out. We walk by the piece of litter on the street, we fail to hold a door open when someone is close behind, or we neglect to ask a child what is wrong when they appear sad or withdrawn.

As a culture we're proud of how casual we can be, when in part we are merely cloaking our apathy. We're told and trained to "stop acting so important." We routinely put others who act from a sense of self-worth in their place by saying things like, "Who do you think you are?" "You're too big for your britches," and "Don't get a big head." It requires courage to break this rule and fully assume our significance without backing down. Excellence requires that we remain present and remember that everything we do or neglect to do has an effect.

☆

THE FIFTH ACTION OF **INTELLIGENT MISBEHAVIOR** IS:

Act Important

Paying Attention to Details

In high school I worked for a local mall, performing mostly as a clown on weekends but occasionally serving other functions in the entertainment of shoppers and especially of their children.

One year the marketing director of the mall approached me and asked if I would like to play Santa Claus for their December Christmas promotion. I was seventeen at the time, and after deciding that it would be fun and a great challenge, I faced the task of transforming myself as realistically as possible from a lean teen to a plump and rosy octogenarian. I took portraying the character seriously and made quite an effort to supplement a basic outfit from the local costume shop with enough strategically placed pillows, pieces of foam, and appropriate makeup to play the part convincingly.

The most fun element of the event was the planned entrance. The mall had arranged with a local helicopter pilot to fly me from a private takeoff point at the city's airport directly to the shopping center, where I would land in the parking lot and hop off to greet any patrons that might assemble.

The day arrived, and the thrill of the helicopter ride over my small town had me already wide-eyed in fascination with the flight, but my eyes grew wider still when we reached the mall and I looked down into the parking lot that had been cleared and cordoned off for the landing. Thousands of children had gathered for "Santa's" arrival. I could hardly believe the turnout, and suddenly I felt quite nervous about who and what I was representing.

Over the course of the day that followed on the Santa throne, I had more children, and a few adults, sit on my lap than I could possibly recount. The idea of Santa to us as adults is, of course, in the realm of whimsy. But the children who jumped up on my knee believed in this symbol of goodness, kindness, charity and cheer, and brought their innocence, vulnerability, and sincerity to my chair. For them, this was no casual event.

I was glad I had taken my uniform seriously, as many of the older children especially were piercing in both their visual and verbal examination of me, making sure I really was Santa. I won the faith and conviction of the vast majority of them and had the privilege of observing the power of their intensity, passion, and imagination.

My experience put a Santa I saw later that month in another location in perspective. The man who had been hired was stopping for regular cigarette breaks between child visits, made no effort to conceal his own dark hair beneath his wig, and evidently considered quick turnaround time to be the priority of his position. The children were having their pictures taken, but the mood of most of them as they walked away was dispirited, disillusioned, or outright alarmed. One child even cried his way out of the Christmas corral.

The popularity of the saying, "God is in the details," arises from a common understanding that details are important. Our attentiveness and responsiveness to them is certainly a vital component of excellence. Tucking in our shirt can land us a job. Signaling a turn in traffic can prevent an accident. Smiling at a stranger can save a pet, or even a child, from being abused at the end of the day.

The conditioning of our culture weakens our presence with distractions. When our attention becomes fleeting and dull, we're expertly prepared to channel surf but ill-equipped to be aware of the present details of our lives. We could say that a "casualty" is anything that perishes due to our inattention to detail, whether it is an opportunity, a personal value, or the spirit of another human being.

Paying attention to the small daily details of our lives is one facet of excellence. When we ignore those details, we discount our ability to make a tangible difference in the lives of others and ourselves.

Providing Witness

Years ago, when I was training to perform an exceptionally difficult juggling trick, I'd often spend many hours a day practicing. One day a neighborhood boy, no more than six, hopped off his bicycle to watch me practice in the front yard. I was there for three hours, and so was the boy. He sat on the curb on the opposite side of the quiet street, his small legs crossed beneath him, an attentive witness of my efforts.

When I finally finished and began packing up my gear, this little sandy-haired kid skipped across the street, walked up to me, and wordlessly began digging around in his pocket. Eventually, he produced one shiny nickel, which he handed to me with a big smile, and again skipped away.

Children are keen observers of the world around them. They have natural presence. They gravitate to the activity of watching others do things that are beyond their skill level. They observe every move, registering patterns, nuances, and details that they will eventually recall when they have the opportunity to try the activity themselves.

While this small boy remained focused on my practice out of a natural urge to learn and grow, it is equally notable that his presence improved the quality of my practice that day. Human attention is powerful. Without having to offer anything beyond the power of our witness, we can make a difference in the outcome of an activity just by being truly present for it. When we offer ourselves as a witness to any human endeavor, we bring out the best in the one doing it. The principle holds true whether we want to support another person or simply wish to bring greater effectiveness to our own personal efforts.

Vince Lombardi is often credited with having said, "Practice does not make perfect. Only perfect practice makes perfect." The difference between practice and perfect practice rests in our ability to observe and witness. We can practice repeatedly to improve at an activity, but if we're only going through the motions without applying attention to our efforts, we are unlikely to make much progress. We may actually reinforce and entrench poor performance habits by practicing inattentively.

In the midst of our busy lives, where speed more often wins out over presence, what is valued is the ability to multitask. What this unfortunately boils down to is how many things we can do inattentively at the same time. We break the rule that says we should pretend we don't matter when we do just one thing with our full attention, making our best effort with a sincere intention for improvement. Once an activity has been mastered and its performance has been reliably perfected, we can think about doing other things at the same time. Take the advice of this juggler, who once tried to tie his shoelace without first getting off his tall unicycle. It was a painful lesson. Sometimes it's best to do one thing at a time with full attention.

Presence and observation give us the information we need to modify and adjust our efforts to make them useful. When we provide witness to others who are practicing to improve at any activity, we communicate and affirm their importance and can help them to find their best effort.

Giving What We Have to Offer

It is practically universal that the observers of my waiter routine register my odd behavior and come to the conclusion that I'm in need of some kind of help. Any real or practical help, however, is rarely provided. When it does come, it comes in the form of aggression or intervention, such as was provided by the psychiatrist whose story I shared in chapter one.

Most people will elect to stay out of the way when confronted by obvious need, and it seems to stem from a sense of insignificance. We apparently feel we cannot make much of a difference to others. We believe we don't know how, or that we don't have the right. My waiter routine often becomes a study in the human capacity for inaction and denial in the face of circumstances that are calling for responsiveness.

Such apathy is driven deep into our psyches by television. We live as though all that happens around us is no more than entertainment—a channel on a remote screen that we can turn on or off. We consider our participation irrelevant, as though we exist in a separate world.

I once performed in Charleston, North Carolina, for a company that holds an annual event to promote a periodical they publish for the restaurant industry. There was a wide range of food industry executives in attendance. Some were menu planners for major restaurant chains across North America and the rest were bulk food suppliers who marketed their products to the menu planners.

Meetings and conferences having to do with the food service industry are always especially fertile ground for my waiter routine, since individuals in that sector are hyperalert and extremely sensitive to food service protocols. At this event, corporate executives of national food service chains were all engaged in socializing and networking as I circulated from table to table in my usual inept manner. They were becoming increasingly more impatient with my incompetence, while simultaneously ignoring the simple and obvious things they could do to make a difference, like offer a kind word or demonstrate a little patience.

There was one man in the room who defied this rule-bound

behavior. He was sitting toward the back of the hall at a table with ten other guests. After I had made several visits to his table, I noticed that he was examining me with a discerning eye. I thought he had figured out that I was an act. As I approached him to replenish his water, pouring from a height of about eighteen inches above the glass and filling it so full it formed a meniscus on the surface, he turned toward me to speak.

Noticing his name tag, I saw that Larry was from Texas. If I had passed the man on the street, I would most likely have summed him up as the product of a "good ol' boy" southern upbringing and wallpapered him with my own set of judgments and biases. Yet, what he said to me in no way corresponded to my prejudice. He proceeded quietly and without fanfare to let me know what a good job I was doing—in a way that was as affirming as it was sincere.

"You know what, Malcolm?" he began (referring to my own fake name tag), "You are doing a *wonderful* job. You just keep up the good work."

With these few words and the kindness he injected into them, he made it abundantly clear to me that any shortcomings I might be imagining I had were nothing more than a shortage of confidence and that I should borrow his confidence in me without delay, relax into my natural abilities, and believe in my adequacy to the task at hand.

On my second trip to his table, when I dropped some silverware on the floor, he once again made the effort to encourage me, saying, "Thank you for taking such good care of us. Just relax. Everyone has a bad day once in a while."

Not only was Larry aware that I was struggling, he put himself in my shoes and realized right away that what he could offer was his belief in my significance. Not only did he indicate that I mattered, he demonstrated his own significance in the process, and silence was not an option in light of it.

In this moment I was taken out of the driver's seat in my role as trickster and entertainer. I was no longer in control of the hand. His kindness and sincerity trumped my cards. He had initiated his own game, and I was scrambling to meet a new mark: human decency. I had been touched, softened, and lifted up because one out of several hundred human beings was not being resigned about his presence in life. He had been paying attention to the details of his circumstance and gave what he had to offer. He was aware of and responsible for his own relevance to the situation at hand.

The next time I returned, Larry addressed the reactions the other guests at his table were having to me by saying, "Don't worry about these people. They're just wound a little too tight. You're doing a great job."

Larry continued this elegant support throughout the entire meal, meeting every attempt I made to deliver inept service with some form of encouragement or empowerment. He spared no effort to communicate to me that I ought to be 100 percent okay with exactly who I was: a significant human being.

I continued the waiter routine through to its programmed crescendo—a final crash, head over heels, with a tray full of metal plate-warmer covers, followed by what is presumably going to be an apology to the guests.

At this point in my act—shuffling, staring at the floor, clearing my throat nervously—I take to the stage, pretending I'm about to apologize. Before the audience knows it, I'm shedding my staff uniform to reveal the blazing colors of my performer's jersey, and the show music for my circus routine is pulsing through the air.

Every time the audience faces this transition, from their belief in my role as an inept waiter to the understanding that I'm actually their entertainment, there is a palpable moment of realization in the room. Along with the external reactions of surprise and delight, there is underneath a trickling river of self-reflection about how easily we ignore what is right in front of us. Since it's all in good fun, there is no lingering sense of offense, only this quick exposure, this passing window to the reality of our casualness and the ease with which we dismiss others in our immediate vicinity.

On this occasion, we all proceeded to have great fun together during the show. I reached the end of the performance, which involves mounting and riding my very tall unicycle. But as I sat perched on top of the unicycle with three hundred people staring upward at me, there was really only one person in my attention. Sitting with dignity in the back of the room was Larry, who had given me more that night than I could offer in return.

My spiel momentarily evaporated, and gesturing toward him, I spoke to the group the only words that remained available to me. "Ladies and gentlemen, Larry is an incredibly kind man." There was no joke, not the setup and punch line I'd trained them to expect, just a simple statement that rode out on a wave of sincerity he himself had engendered and which, in the dark, I could only hope he accepted.

An awards ceremony for the members of this association

followed the conclusion of my show. Once the awards had finished, the guests began to mingle. Many visited for quite some time, while others departed leisurely from the room.

After everyone had left the ballroom and I stood alone near the stage packing up my equipment, I looked up to see Larry reenter through the far doors and slowly make his way toward me across the hall, a very sober expression on his face. Saying nothing, he simply walked over to me and pulled up a chair. I sat down as well, as he clearly had a reason for returning to see me.

A building tension played around his jaw, while his eyes flashed with mixed emotion. He appeared to be tender, appreciative, and disturbed all at the same time. He began speaking to me about his children—his son and particularly his daughter, a fourteen-year-old who had been diagnosed several years earlier with a life-threatening illness. She wanted to give up, and he had elected to quit his job as an executive chef to be her full-time support.

He spoke of how difficult it was to support his daughter when she was embittered and bewildered by the injustice of her condition. On top of her situation, the man struggled to attend to the challenges of parenting a teenage son as well. He talked about being a father, about its challenges—and he talked about the pain of not measuring up to what he saw was needed, of not being able to make it all better.

He began to openly weep.

He didn't cover his face. He didn't hide, didn't shrink from those tears, but looked at me and let the waters of his breaking heart wash down on his suit and tie. Then he said, "I've never had more doubts about myself as a father and a person than I have in the last two years. I had no idea tonight that you were an entertainer and not a real waiter, but because of what you did," he said, his voice choked with emotion, "I got to see that who I am is a *good* person."

He stood up, came to where I sat, and kissed me on the top of my head before walking out.

That's the last time I ever saw or spoke to Larry, but I have told his story to others again and again because his courage and dignity are something I still feel, and his example deserves to be shared. This man, who had actively empowered the significance of another human being, created for himself a context that reflected his own merit, his consequence as an individual, and his value in the world.

When we stop pretending that we do not matter, we retain the power to champion the significance of others.

Accountability

When the fifth rule is operating unconsciously in us, we are not only limited in our personal ability to engage excellence, we also disempower those around us. This is magnified many times if we are operating as an authority figure in a group dynamic.

I once worked for a client whose meeting was being held at a large and well-known resort. The banquet captain who had been assigned to oversee the servers for this particular group had been newly promoted to the post. It was evident that he was reluctant to take charge of his large group of servers. The mood among the servers was relaxed and jovial, yet lacked the backbone of clear direction. The freshly installed banquet captain was unable to connect with his own importance. The casualness with which he fulfilled his function translated into lackluster service on the part of the entire staff, and the delivery of the client company's meal was slow and problematic.

During that evening, one of the servers who was a new recruit at the hotel spilled some water in the service hallway and neglected to attend immediately to mopping it up. A veteran server, unaware of the spill, walked into the puddle. He slipped, fell, and had to be taken to the hospital on a stretcher.

A connection to our significance sets the tone for others to realize their own relevance to the circumstance at hand and to take responsibility for their actions. Acting with a healthy sense of our importance creates accountability in our organizations.

CHAPTER 5 SUMMARY

THE FIFTH RULE WE WERE BORN TO BREAK IS:

Pretend You Don't Matter

THE FIFTH MISBEHAVIOR IS:

Act Important

THE BENEFIT OF BREAKING THIS RULE IN A GROUP IS:

Accountability

Every person impacts his or her environment and therefore automatically makes a difference. The conditioned sense that we do not matter disconnects us from the experience of being significant and able to make a positive difference in our world. The misbehavior that defies the invitation to tune out and give up is to *act important*.

Paying Attention to Details

Often, if a small child is assigned a task and asked to help, they will carry out the request in earnest. To a child, every moment counts because they intuitively sense that they are representatives of life's necessity to evolve and optimize itself through every being, interaction, and occurrence. All phenomena have meaning and purpose. All elements of life arise with the potential to transform the world in some way. A child's innate connection to this law is the basis of an acute attention to detail that is pure and natural and is the fundamental quality we can connect with to improve our performance in any area of life.

Providing Witness

Our presence alone has worth. The power of our witness can provide energy, encouragement, comfort, and support to others. Nonjudgmental observation of our own states, behaviors, and feelings provides us with clarity and perspective about ourselves. To be present as a witness of one's own activities is an essential component in any quest for excellence.

Giving What We Have to Offer

Giving to others what we have to offer often has the surprising result of providing us with exactly what we need as well. This is because the process of providing value to others makes our own strengths undeniable. If we refrain from giving what we have to offer, we can easily forget the virtues and capacities we possess. When we champion others to be their best, we remind ourselves of our potential and lift ourselves into the realm of excellence.

The difference we can make in our own lives and in the lives of others when we remain present to details, witness, and give what we have to offer is beyond our knowing. We certainly don't discover it when we take a backseat in a world that is full of possibility and potential.

The truth is, we cannot be insignificant. Our presence in life, whether we step forward and contribute or withhold and doubt the value of what we have to offer, has an impact on others and on our environments. When we see past our discounting of ourselves, embrace our significance, and are willing to act in response, life turns into a series of small and sometimes even large miracles and wonders.

Accountability characterizes the climate within a group when its members remain connected to their significance, realize their own relevance to the circumstance at hand, and take responsibility for their actions.

PRETEND YOU DON'T MATTER
is the fifth rule we were born to break.

STAY IN CONTROL

THE DYNAMICS OF CONTROL VERSUS relationship is a central theme of everything from the greatest of classical literature to the best of our Hollywood films. The classic story, *A Christmas Carol*, that features the character of Scrooge delights us because we see the transformation of a man whose impulse to be in control matures into the desire to honor and protect his relationships.

While some of the best stories feature such a transformation, some of the most poignant portray the failure of it, as in William Shakespeare's tragic *Romeo and Juliet*, where two lovers from warring families are caught in a cross fire of intolerance and prejudice. Such a depiction leaves us with the bitter reflection that our unwillingness to see the other's point of view has less than favorable—and often tragic—consequences.

Ultimately, we cannot control other people. The belief that we need to control others to achieve our aims only distances them from us, and on some occasions compels those who could help us to instead actively oppose us.

> *I argue very well. Ask any of my remaining friends. I can win any argument on any topic. People know this and steer clear of me at parties. Often, as a sign of their great respect, they don't even invite me.*
>
> DAVE BARRY

When we acknowledge others as distinct human beings, when we truly see and make the effort to understand them, they feel received, honored, and respected. This acknowledgement of others is the very basis of our capacity to enjoy powerful and mutually fulfilling relationships.

THE SIXTH ACTION OF **INTELLIGENT MISBEHAVIOR** IS:

Build Relationship

Forgiving and Forgetting

In the earlier days of my street performing career it was not uncommon for me to see various celebrities in my audience. Vancouver, which has been dubbed "Hollywood of the North" because of the number of feature films produced there, is no stranger to visiting celebrities. Since the Public Market in Vancouver is a tourist destination, it draws stars as well as the general public. Over the years I saw quite a few familiar faces. Hal Holbrook, Paula Abdul, Emilio Estevez, and Donny Osmond were a few I recognized.

In the summer of 1987, the movie *The Untouchables* had just been released, starring, among others, Robert De Niro, Sean Connery, Kevin Costner, and Charles Martin Smith. Mr. Smith had by then appeared in films such as *Never Cry Wolf*, which he had starred in several years earlier, *American Graffiti*, and *The Buddy Holly Story* in the 1970s. I recognized him immediately when he showed up in the audience at one of my public shows with a small group of friends.

At the time, I had a routine that involved juggling a bowling ball, a toilet plunger, and a ping-pong ball. It involved a fair bit of audience participation that led up to the actual juggling of the items. The plunger, I had discovered, would stick nicely atop any head of an audience member who was follically challenged. Mr. Smith fit the category.

I remember pegging his shiny pate with the plunger and using the secure fit to lead him onstage while holding the plunger handle. The audience, as you can imagine, roars at the outrageousness of this bit, no matter who the victim is.

I don't know how many people recognized who my volunteer actually was. The only thing I clearly remember is Mr. Smith's bearing. He didn't resist, nor did he ham it up in any way. He just maintained utter composure, even with a plunger on his head. He simply accepted this role that I had cast him in and walked away with quiet humility and self-respect once the whole routine was over.

I recall what a profound impact Mr. Smith's example made upon me. Without saying a word, he communicated volumes. The first message was, Keep your dignity. Whatever you're doing, make sure it is not beneath your own or another's dignity to engage it. The second message was, Forgive and move on. There is no benefit to breaching relationship in order to be right. The offer of dignity and presence alone will allow others to see their mistakes and correct them without having to start an argument or make them pay.

Much of what happens on stage with comedy centers around the dynamic of control. Pasting the plunger on a human being's head and leading them on stage is an exaggeration of what we will resort to in the effort to control. Mr. Smith's response, however, which was completely without antagonism or reaction, made him the authority in this circumstance. He engaged me in relationship with his bearing and his presence. As he walked away, I felt connected to him. I wanted to apologize or make amends.

I never did get the chance, as I was in the middle of my show and he left soon afterward. Understandably. If you happen to know Mr. Smith personally, please convey my apologies and let him know that the juggler on Granville Island who once stuck a plunger on his head is sorry for going a little too far.

We protect our relationships when we forgive transgressions and give the other party enough room to consider and reflect upon their own behavior rather than demanding retribution or making sure they know they are wrong.

Honoring the Truth of Others

Street performers are often faced with some of the same crowd dynamics that riot police use tear gas to deal with. The term "crowd control" is equally as relevant to the open-air performer as it is to law enforcement professionals. How a performer remains in charge of an audience, however, must obviously depend upon connection, competent engagement, and finesse rather than force.

One of my street show routines involves obtaining a male volunteer from the audience to help me with a juggling stunt. Running into the crowd at one performance, I selected the man I wanted to join me up front. I picked him because he had an obviously impressive physique, which is important for the success of the bit. Though large and well proportioned, he resisted my invitation, but he fit what I needed so precisely that I forced the issue and led the assembled crowd in a chant that didn't abate until he agreed to come up and participate. He finally relented and reluctantly came to the front with me.

For this routine, once I have the volunteer on stage, I move close and indicate through my body language that he looks tense and needs to relax, to loosen up. I dodge behind him and massage his shoulders as if he were a prize fighter between rounds. Generally, I pick a volunteer who seems withdrawn at first, as once this type of person comes out of their shell the audience responds with great delight in witnessing the conversion. This particular audience member didn't appear to be warming to the theatrics.

The next part of the interaction involves my enticing the volunteer to copy my actions as I loosely shake my hands, arms, and then face, presumably to relax and let the tension go. This he did, but without much enthusiasm. I then lift my arms in the air with an expectant look, at which point the participant usually responds by stretching up in the same way. Then, in one deft motion, I reach down, grab the tails of the man's T-shirt, lift it up over his head and arms and off his body in a blink. This is why I always pick a man who has a good build. The vast majority of the time the volunteer takes it in good stride, often actually enjoying the attention of getting to flex his stuff in front of a crowd.

On this day, however, I had simply forced the circumstance. Not wanting to be there at all, this volunteer looked at me blankly—and I at him. "Can I have my shirt back now?" he said, finding none of the amusement in it that was intended. I prompted the audience to give the man a huge hand for sticking it out, and he quickly left the stage and disappeared into the crowd.

The nature of such live theater on the street is that things don't always work. You do your best in such instances and move on. That's show business.

I went to my prop case to get the equipment I needed for the next routine, the juggling of five balls. After gathering them in my hands, I turned toward the audience, my back now to the case. In the meantime, unbeknownst to me, the volunteer I had just dismissed had circled around the outskirts of the crowd and snuck up behind me past the prop case at my back. Before I was aware of his presence, he silently moved close enough to grab the bottom hem of my shorts on each leg and drop them briskly to my ankles.

As my volunteer darted away, I was left exposed in a living version of the common naked-in-a-crowd nightmare.

There were the guffaws of those who were buckled over in laughter, delighted with my volunteer's revenge, and there was the shock of those who had absolutely no idea how to handle the entire episode. These people were so distraught they had to physically depart from the area, looking at the ground and mumbling in an attempt to process what they had just seen.

I reached down and pulled up my shorts, tightening the drawstring in a way that got another good laugh. Once that was done, I flung my arms open in my best circus form and flashed a big-finish grin at those assembled, with a "TA-DAH!" thrown in for good measure, even though in actuality I have never been more embarrassed in my life.

The incident taught me to be more responsive to the state of my volunteers and to make sure that my connection to and respect of them is the priority.

It all comes down to our willingness to consider the other person's perspective, to take a breath in the midst of our agenda and consider the truth of the person we're dealing with. To exercise control in the absence of connection eventually results in the loss of control, since it's only a matter of time before someone who goes unacknowledged and is left disconnected finds an opportunity to counter our will with their own.

Many of us in leadership positions hold the belief that control must be maintained to avoid the breakdown of the structures we are responsible for—our families, companies, or communities—and that to open ourselves to others' points of view would be to weaken our authority. Unquestionably, it is important that we maintain our authority as parents of our children and as leaders of the organizations and businesses we serve. Yet, there is a crucial distinction to be made between the natural influence we enjoy through relationship and the control we are forced to resort to in its absence.

To misbehave in relationship to our cultural conditioning around the issue of control is to acknowledge and honor the truth of others and to connect with them prior to trying to direct them.

Including Others

I was once performing at a corporate event in Naples, Florida, at the Ritz Carlton Hotel. It was a classy black-tie awards banquet for a professional association. I had finished the waiter routine and begun my stage show for this large group of corporate executives. The show was unfolding beautifully.

Then, suddenly, somewhere in the middle of the crowd, a cell phone rang.

This happens sometimes. People forget to turn them off or put them on mute. Generally, I ignore the intrusion, but in this instance the owner of the phone, an elderly woman who was the wife of one of the executives, answered it and began a spirited conversation with somebody on the other end that was quite audible to everyone in the audience. As everyone knows, in comedy timing is everything. The sequence of elements I had been delicately structuring to bring this entire presentation to a glorious and captivating finale came to a grinding halt.

I stopped what I was doing onstage and gave the woman a long, comically disbelieving look. It had no effect, as she was too engrossed in her conversation to notice. Even as everyone was laughing at her obliviousness, she continued her dialogue in tones that indicated the call's importance to her. She seemed to be debating something with someone, and it was evident that she wasn't going to stop talking.

I felt angry and wanted to control her behavior, yet I knew that getting aggressive in response would have been no less of an interruption. I had to broaden the boundaries of my plans for a successful show; otherwise, it was simply going to get away from me. So I decided to connect by investigating the importance of this conversation to her. I walked off the stage and threaded my way through a few of the tables to where she was sitting. Finally she looked up, and for the first time realized the attention she had drawn to herself.

I reached down and gently removed the phone from her hand, holding it up to my ear so I could speak to whoever was on the line. I also lifted the lapel microphone I was wearing to the phone speaker so the audience could be privy to the conversation.

I began by introducing myself and asking to whom I was speaking. We heard a man's voice reply. Punctuated by chuckles, he told us he was the woman's son. Evidently, having reached her boy on the line, this concerned mother didn't want to let him go, despite the inappropriateness of the circumstances under which she was chatting. Perhaps it had been some time since they spoke. It may even have been that he was avoiding her. The tone we all overheard in the mother's voice was the mood of an anxious parent.

I explained to the son that his mother was in the middle of a live theater performance and suggested that the call could be resumed at a later time. The son told the listening crowd and me that he understood completely. Since the moment early in the call when his mother had mentioned where she was, he had been trying to convince her to hang up the phone. This is apparently what they were debating about. His urge for her to end the call was based on the fact that he himself was a comedian, a successful stand-up living in New York City. He had been telling his mother that if she didn't get off the phone she would be singled out and would soon find herself part of the performance.

Needless to say, this episode was the highlight of the entire evening. Nothing I could have planned in advance or enforced with respect to my idea of a perfect show could have matched the entertainment value of what had been accessed outside of the demand for control.

Our lives are full of ordinary moments in relationship where we are required to take charge in some way, but we must learn to do it without alienating those whom we need to guide, lead, or work with. Often when we are frustrated by someone's lack of compliance with our program, we simply want to eliminate them, excluding them from participating if they won't do it our way. Excluding and eliminating, however, does not solve the problem, nor does it enhance our authority in the eyes of those who have to continue working with us.

It is only through skillful connection, founded on a true interest in including others, that we open the door for excellence.

Leadership

Leaders give priority to relationship rather than relying on methods of imposed control to achieve organizational aims. We all, from time to time, are called to function in leadership capacities. Sometimes we are formally acknowledged in our leadership roles. On other occasions we have to be aware enough to realize that we have a responsibility to an informal position of leadership.

As I've mentioned, years ago I toured in New Zealand and Australia to street perform. After visiting and working in Melbourne, Sydney, and Brisbane, I crossed the vast country with my then girlfriend and traveling partner to finish our tour in Perth.

We enthusiastically jumped into the busking scene and did exceptionally well. As we continued to offer shows, we became increasingly popular with the locals and were making quite good money. My visibility as a performer was high, not only with the local patrons of the mall where we were stationed, but also with the other entertainers. In enjoying the audience responses we were getting I had neglected to make any strong connections with the rest of the performer community. I had even used my success as a way to throw my weight around, subtly leveraging my way into as many prime performance slots as I could.

Under the circumstances, I had a responsibility to make real connections with the other performers. I possessed a natural authority within the informal system of entertainers. By the time

I realized the need to make this connection it was too late. Another entertainer had already called Australian immigration to tip them off about a foreign worker who was conducting business without a work visa. It brought our performances there to an abrupt end and we opted to leave town prior to any trouble. Our personal opportunity as well as the chance to strengthen the street-performing community through attention to relationship had been lost.

Leadership arises out of strong connections and relationships and requires that we break the rule of staying in control within our organizations.

CHAPTER 6 SUMMARY

THE SIXTH RULE WE WERE BORN TO BREAK IS:

Stay in Control

THE SIXTH MISBEHAVIOR IS:

Build Relationships

THE BENEFIT OF BREAKING THIS RULE IN A GROUP IS:

Leadership

Connections are the key to success. The notion that we ought to be able to control others and force their obedience only undermines our ability to be close to and cooperate with those we share our homes or workplaces with. The misbehavior that allows us to rise above this rule is to *build relationships*.

Forgiving and Forgetting

There is no benefit to be gained in breaching relationship in order to be right. The offer of dignity and presence alone will allow others to see their mistakes and correct them without having to start an argument or make them pay. We protect our relationships when we forgive transgressions and give the other party enough room to consider and reflect upon their own behavior rather than demanding retribution or making sure they know they are wrong.

Honoring the Truth of Others

The cultivation of relationship requires receptivity—our openness to the person we are relating to. If we're in the habit of jumping to conclusions about others and making assumptions about them, it will be difficult to see them as they are. We cannot enter into a powerful connection with someone if we do not see things from their point of view. Putting our own agenda aside is essential if we hope to form an alliance with them.

Including Others

Our lives are full of ordinary moments in relationship where we are required to take charge in some way, but we must learn to do it without alienating others. Often when we're frustrated by someone's lack of compliance with our program, we simply want to eliminate them, excluding them from participating if they won't do it our way. Excluding and eliminating, however, doesn't solve the problem, nor does it enhance our authority in the eyes of those who remain in our circle. It is only through skillful connection, founded on a true interest in including others, that we open the door for excellence.

When we are willing to let go of the conditioned need for control that we cling to in many situations and open ourselves to relationship, we become an active contributor to everyone's potential for excellence.

Leadership results when group members give priority to relationship rather than relying on methods of imposed control to achieve organizational aims.

STAY IN CONTROL
is the sixth rule we were born to break.

7

BE POPULAR

WE LOOK UP TO AND ADMIRE THE mastery of talented and accomplished individuals. An increasing exposure to media, however, means we are more and more impacted by the packaged personas of celebrities, sports heroes, and public figures.

Today we face the stark discrepancy between the attention that is given to the stars of our culture and the interest we generate from others in our own lives. We do not create the kind of responses that Eminem, Brad Pitt, or Mariah Carey earn, of course, yet we're conditioned to believe we should.

We live with the contrast between our own experience and

the cultural idolization of marketed heroes. Imagining that celebrities are satisfied and happy, we start thinking that we will experience fulfillment also if we become popular.

> *I used to compete in sports, and then I realized: You can buy trophies. Now I'm good at everything.*
>
> DEMETRI MARTIN

The conditioned pursuit of popularity undermines our excellence as we abandon our authentic talents, interests, and potential to adopt styles and attitudes that are not really ours, or strive for notoriety through activities that are foreign to us.

When we invest in popular opinions, we can sacrifice our personal dignity, dismiss invaluable sources of guidance, and lose touch with the inner victories that are the hallmark and guiding force of excellence.

☆

THE SEVENTH ACTION OF **INTELLIGENT MISBEHAVIOR** IS:

Follow a Vision

Ignoring Armchair Critics

Many years ago I was contacted by the Fort St. John Oilman's Association in the far north of British Columbia, Canada, about an event they were planning. They required entertainment for

five hundred association members—oil field and rig workers—
for their winter celebration. A contract was signed, and before
I knew it I was bouncing way up north on a little prop plane to
the small, snowy town where the sun shines for about six hours
a day in the winter months.

My performance would take place at the local high school on
the stage that was at one end of the cafeteria following the group's
celebration dinner. I stood ready behind the red velvet curtain
as the announcement was made that it was time for the evening's
entertainment. The men were full of energy, excited, and vocally
enthusiastic, until the emcee asked them to put their hands
together for juggler Rick Lewis.

No one had bothered to mention to me that the only form
of entertainment provided to this group in the previous twenty
years had involved a boom box and a person of the opposite sex
trained in the slow and methodic removal of various pieces of
clothing.

The curtain went up as the loud booing of the crowd filled
the entire auditorium. I stood there as they jeered, wondering
what would happen next. From halfway to the back of the hall,
one of the men threw his spoon, which landed with a ping on
the wooden stage where I was standing. There was a pause, and
a moment later several hundred more spoons were launched into
the air, like shrapnel from an exploding bomb.

The spoons clattered to stillness on the stage, and then all the
men went silent, waiting to see what I would do.

Life is full of such moments, though mostly not quite so
dramatic, where we are faced with the choice between caving in
to criticism and disapproval by modifying what we stand for or

sticking with what we believe in and letting others take it or leave it. When we respond from a connection to our vision as opposed to lowering ourselves to the conditioned standards of the crowd, it commands authority because we demonstrate the courage that all people wish for themselves: to stay the course with what we authentically have to offer to the world.

This is, of course, much easier to talk about than it is to do when we're faced with such a moment, as I was there on the cafeteria stage. I remember my heart pounding and my mind racing, looking for an option as to how to proceed. I knew that if I panicked in the face of their taunt, I would have no chance of being able to proceed with the show. I had no more than a few seconds to communicate who I was and what I had to offer. After that, it was anyone's guess what behavior these men, out of their crowd mentality, would indulge.

In that moment, I connected to a sense of pride and the value I knew I could offer. I stared out at the audience and let the tension of the moment linger as the crowd waited to see how I would react to their demonstration. Then I suddenly sprang into the air, performed a full backflip, feet to feet, and again stood still, looking out at the crowd.

There was another moment of silence before the entire group erupted into applause and cheers. I had earned a green light and was able to successfully complete the performance.

In retrospect, I saw that this group had been asked on the spot to leave a long-standing tradition behind and accept something entirely new. They were disappointed. Their display of protest was a demand that approval for this different direction be earned.

If we have an inspiration for something new, we're going to face such challenges from others who will disapprove and threaten to stop liking us if we insist on a change. To stand our ground, ignore armchair critics, and communicate our vision is an important capacity if we wish to move toward excellence.

Looking Up to Masters

After high school, I was accepted to and attended Webster University in St. Louis for two years of university education. Webster is a liberal arts college with a highly respected theater program. My dream at the time was to become an actor, yet just getting into this program was highly competitive, and all applicants were required to audition. The program's style was professionally oriented immersion training; we breathed, ate and slept theater 24/7. Producing reputable actors for legitimate work in the entertainment industry was the focus, and there was a casting board for professional performing jobs where both national and local St. Louis opportunities were posted.

I hadn't been at the university for more than a week when a casting call for musical theater talent went up for a new Dr. Pepper commercial. It was during the 1970s that Dr. Pepper introduced a commercial style that was staged like a production number from a Broadway musical. A series of these commercials starring David Naughton became very popular for the brand.

It is well known among actors and performers in the industry that landing a national commercial for a recognized brand can be one of the most lucrative forms of income for an actor. These jobs not only pay a reasonable sum initially, they can also bring significant residual payments for many years, depending on how frequently the spots are shown.

Thrilled at the chance of getting such work, I jumped into a van of sophomores and juniors who were answering the casting call and stood in line with several hundred other dancers to audition. Over the course of many hours, the casting directors and producers began weeding out candidates by watching us dance in large groups. As the afternoon wore on, I was thrilled to still be on their list, dancing with two other groups of six or seven people on the way to a total of ten being selected. The short story is that I was offered a part as a "pepper."

When I returned to the school ready to boast about having just been validated by a popular offshoot of the entertainment industry, I was quickly told by one of my instructors about the very strict no-performance policy that applied to freshmen students. The stance of the school was that the freshman year of theater conservatory was chiefly for the purpose of reversing the bad performance habits that inevitably accompanied all who entered the program and that a hiatus from performing was essential while new habits were being introduced and practiced. I was given an option: take the role and quit the school, or turn down the offer and remain with the program.

My decision to remain in the conservatory was a difficult one, but without doubt the right choice. What I learned from a host of other professional actors, voice coaches, and movement teachers has been of supreme value to me in my work as an entertainer. I draw upon the fundamentals I learned there every time I perform.

There is no doubt that taking the commercial would have led to some degree of notoriety, yet such public appeal in no way guarantees us a relationship to disciplines and practices of excellence that will allow us to keep growing and developing. Webster University understood the distinction that we have failed to make in our culture between popular acclaim and the presence of true guidance, and it was the choice to engage the presence of a gifted teaching staff that set me on a course that had true potential.

Pursuing Dreams

I've been trying to get laughs for as long as I can remember. From plays and skits in elementary school to clowning in high school to serious acting in university, the desire to entertain has never waned. By the time I left college I had lots of experience in front of audiences, but I still had an unrealized dream to street perform. The immediacy, freedom, and challenge of a completely unregulated performance venue fascinated me.

At the age of twenty I moved to a small town a few hours' drive from Portland, Oregon. Determined to finally try busking, I spent months developing my first street show, which consisted of mime routines, juggling, and magic tricks. When I felt I was ready, I went to Portland to look for a venue. I discovered Jefferson Square, an open plaza surrounded by office buildings that at lunchtime emptied of workers who grabbed deli fare and sat on the steps of the plaza to eat and socialize. It was an ideal spot to try my first street show.

The weather was perfect—a sunny, warm fall afternoon. Two hundred people sat in tiers around the plaza center as I strode to what I would use as my stage area right in front of the steps.

I was dressed in a colorful mime costume complete with white-face. There was no place for me to hide and no half way to do it. It was clear what I was there to do.

I set down my prop bag and began.

I had been extremely nervous prior to the show. Once I started, however, I was quickly able to focus my energy and get into a flow. I relaxed. The show unfolded effortlessly and I easily recalled the sequence of my first routine, though I had been afraid I would forget it. It all felt great.

At the end of that first routine, I stopped and looked up at the audience in anticipation of their applause and appreciation. What I discovered instead was that not a single person among the hundreds gathered on those steps had stopped eating or talking for a moment to give me even the slightest bit of attention. They were unapologetically in a flow of their own that intersected in no way with mine.

My heart stopped. I felt the warm flush of embarrassment and the urge to grab my things and run. Then, in the midst of my desire to vanish, it dawned on me that this was as bad as it could get. I realized then that I could survive the absence of popularity. In the course of less than a minute I discovered my own love for my craft, and a shift happened for me on that day that has never left. I realized that it was more important for me to do what I loved to do than it was to be acknowledged for it. I had found a healthy distance from the opinions of others by pursuing my dream.

I felt a huge weight lift off me. Since the worst thing had already happened, there was nothing that could stop me from continuing. I finished the remainder of my show that day without the least bit of appreciation. I took a big, slow bow anyway, and walked away with supreme gratitude for what that experience provided—the realization of how essential my love for live performance actually was and the understanding that nothing could stop me from one day doing it well.

When we pursue a vision and experience the fulfillment that accompanies our dedication to it, we discover that victory is something we can experience whether or not we have an audience. It is true that we can experience a deep sense of purpose and validation when others receive the value we have to offer and are changed or inspired by it. It is the integrity with which we express our vision for excellence, however, that is most important. If we deny, dismiss, or bypass the importance of that vision in a campaign for popularity, we may find that while our audience is growing, what we have to offer is fading away.

Integrity

To champion a vision is often to behave in ways that others may not appreciate or understand in the moment. If being popular is what is most important to us, we may have difficulty guarding the integrity of the organization we wish to serve.

I recently performed as the headline act at the President's Club dinner for a large company in the business of writing mortgages. In attendance were about sixty of this company's most successful salespeople, the backbone of the organization's profitability. After finishing my show, I stood at the back of the room while the president came forward to address these top performers and their attending partners and spouses.

While the event had been a celebration of the group's achieve-
ments and successes, the president's final words were the last
thing I expected to hear, and probably the last thing these employees thought they would hear as well.

The president began by saying how sobered he was to wake
each morning to the reality that his industry and his very own
company had significantly contributed to the economic troubles
now faced by the entire nation. He detailed how his company
had participated in the meltdown of banking institutions and
previously stable financial structures by becoming lax and greedy
in their business. He detailed his responsibility for the problem
and admitted his personal mistakes. He then called for an immediate change in their corporate habits, declaring that the trust
of their customers and the general public had been deservedly
lost and that the vision of their company was to start the following
day to earn it back by being trustworthy and reliable in their
profession.

The result of the success of such a vision would without question bring less cash profit to this organization. The vision, however, focused on another kind of profit: the ensuring of a
sustainable future and the value of human integrity.

I watched as he concluded his speech and walked off the stage
to his seat. As the DJ began playing music and the dance floor
opened up, the group broke into socializing. Not a single
employee came forward to acknowledge or thank this president
for speaking the truth and for leading the way to a more responsible future. He had demonstrated a rare degree of dignity and
courage, yet there was no fanfare, no flurry of acknowledgment.
He simply sat alone with his wife.

For months I kept thinking about his unusually honest and real address. I was curious to find out what had happened. Finally I picked up the phone and called him. He told me that he had barely slept after his speech that night, worried that he had made a big mistake being so forthright and demanding with his team. The anxiety lasted for days, but then an amazing thing happened. He began getting calls from the spouses who were in attendance with their partners, thanking him for the stand he had taken for the organization's integrity. He explained how deeply meaningful this was to him, knowing he had the support of the families who stood behind his employees as they came to work every day.

Leaders who are willing to guard the integrity of an organizational vision eventually create teams and work groups that can move forward with purpose, effectiveness, and clarity. In the early stages of serving such a vision, and sometimes even long after, this requires the ability of a leader to transcend the rule of popularity.

CHAPTER 7 SUMMARY

THE SEVENTH RULE WE WERE BORN TO BREAK IS:

Be Popular

THE SEVENTH MISBEHAVIOR IS:

Follow a Vision

THE BENEFIT OF BREAKING THIS RULE IN A GROUP IS:

Integrity

We are meant to honor our convictions, not the whims of a crowd. The idea that popularity will be fulfilling may entice us to place our commitments aside for immediate recognition or attention. The misbehavior that helps us to move beyond this rule is to *follow a vision*.

Ignoring Armchair Critics

If we have a vision for something new, we're going to face challenges from others who will disapprove and threaten to stop liking us if we insist on a change. To stand our ground, ignore the naysayers, and communicate our vision is an important capacity if we wish to move toward excellence.

Looking Up to Masters

What appears to be popularity is often no more than fleeting approval that is the reflection of a collective whim. Focused on popularity, we may never come into contact with those whose opinions really count. When we seek the guidance of masters, we orient ourselves to the opinions and counsel of those who possess the authority of experience—those whose discrimination has been refined and who can support us to remain committed to a higher vision. These are the individuals who can lead us rightly in our own quest for greatness. We must turn to them so we can continue to grow long after we find ourselves with the broad appeal that brings mainstream success.

Pursuing Our Dreams

When we pursue a vision and experience the fulfillment that accompanies our dedication to it, we discover that victory is something we can experience whether or not we have an audience. It is true that we can experience a deep sense of purpose and validation when others receive what we have to offer and are changed or inspired by it. Yet, it is our steadfast commitment to our vision of excellence that is most important. If we dismiss the importance of that vision looking for popularity, we may find that while our audience grows, what we have to offer fades away.

It is a mistake to allow a desire to be admired to take precedence over our vision or the opportunity to apprentice to any bonafide master. In the words of comedian Tony Follari, "Stardom is seldom the kingdom of freedom." Nor, we could add, of excellence.

Integrity remains protected within an organization when leaders are willing to behave in ways that others may not appreciate or understand in the moment. Such leaders who are willing to stand alone as the champion of an organization's mission eventually create teams and work groups that can move forward with purpose, effectiveness, and clarity.

BE POPULAR
is the seventh rule we were born to break.

☆

THE SEVEN ORGANIZATIONAL
BENEFITS OF RULE BREAKING

WE WERE BORN TO EXCEL. Embedded in our culture, however, is a series of rules that undermine our potential and disempower our orientation to purpose, fulfillment, and happiness.

Just seeing the existence of these rules is an important step in freeing ourselves to live at our best; yet, an acknowledgement and understanding of them alone is not enough. We need consistent and dedicated practice to overcome their influence. Such personal work is essential if we hope to participate effectively in support of the organizations, companies, or causes we believe in. Whether we are part of a family, a church, a business, a community, or an association, we all find ourselves having to navigate the waters of human relationship and group dynamics.

As a meeting presenter, my job is to facilitate successful gatherings—to create an atmosphere of shared enjoyment and the desire to take positive action on behalf of a vision, product, or cause. Due to the relatively brief window I'm given to generate an environment for growth and progress, I've learned to use the breaking of rules as a potent means of activating a group's passion and appetite for action.

While the principles and experiences I've shared in this book can help you to grow personally, they can also assist you to serve as a leader in the groups you care about. Personal excellence and organizational growth are inextricably linked. Organizations are greatly impacted by whether the seven hidden rules are acknowledged and intentionally addressed by its workers or members. A plan of strategic rule breaking is an essential component of organizational success and a task that must be assumed by all leaders, whether they represent a family, a church, a nonprofit association, or a for-profit venture of any size.

Here is a quick reminder and summary for future reference of the seven misbehaviors and their corresponding organizational benefits.

1. The willingness to be *authentic* is the basis of effective **communication**.

2. When an organization's members are supported to *take chances*, **innovation** is not far away.

3. The practice of *asking for help* is the foundation of organizational **teamwork**.

4. When *determination* perhaps even bordering on obsession is encouraged, **productivity** results.

5. Workers who accept their significance and *act important* bring **accountability** to their organization.

6. When *building relationship* is valued over maintaining control, exceptional **leadership** emerges.

7. When those leaders are willing to *follow a vision* rather than cling to popularity, the **integrity** of the organization's vision can be preserved and realized.

9

WHY WE NEED INTELLIGENT
MISBEHAVIOR FOR REAL CHANGE

ENGAGING EXCELLENCE REQUIRES ongoing risk, effort, and persistence. We all possess the capacity for excellence by virtue of being human. The question is, what stops that capacity from becoming reality? Many of our methods of motivating ourselves toward excellence fail to have lasting impact. Why?

Our answer is usually to assume that we are not motivated enough, and so we look for more motivational techniques, systems, and ideas to add to our collection. What I'm suggesting is required is an *antimotivational* process, because it is the *presence of motivations we already have* that prevents our excellence. A lack of motivation is not the problem.

When we say, "I'm not feeling motivated," what we really mean is that we're feeling quite motivated to withhold our passion, veil our truth, sit back and hope that our compliance with the agreements to mediocrity that characterize our culture will magically make our lives work. In short, we are motivated to obey the seven rules.

The hidden motivating forces of our culture suppress our natural capacity for excellence. We disarm the grip of these unconscious patterns by fully understanding where they come from and seeing how they operate in our lives. That's easier said than done, however, because the seven rules are so pervasive that they have become invisible to us.

The rule *be popular*, for example, causes us to invest heavily in products that we hope will change the way others perceive us. Unconscious of what we're doing, we spend billions on objects, status symbols, and activities that offer no real personal satisfaction.

Recently I was watching TV with my teenage son as we sat through a long infomercial aimed at selling hair implants to balding men. The producers interviewed this bald guy who lamented, "I'm so tired of people staring at the top of my head instead of looking me in the face when they're talking to me," as if his baldness was such a distraction it sabotaged potential relationships. I commented to the TV screen, "Dude, maybe it has something to do with your face." This was one of only several moments in the fathering of my teenager when I was considered cool. I got a high five, and then my son said, "Seriously, Dad, maybe you should call them."

It's important for us to recognize that we're trained to try to buy our way into success and happiness. The truth of this conditioning once prompted a famous con man to coin the phrase, "There is a sucker born every minute." We'll even buy things that are clearly not good for us in our desperation for meaning and acceptance.

The most hazardous product we can purchase from our culture, however, is not an SUV, a cell phone, a computer, a weapon, fast food, or toxic chemicals for our lawn. The most dangerous thing we buy wholesale from our culture is its *ideas*.

Try this experiment. Answer the following three questions out loud and without hesitating:

What is the largest appliance in a kitchen?
What is the most common color of this appliance?
What do cows drink?

Each succeeding question sets you up to think "milk" in response to the final question. By using a string of associations, the unconscious expectation was created that reality ought to proceed in a particular direction. It is, of course, of little consequence if we mistakenly think for a moment that cows drink milk instead of water. What makes the exercise alarming is how easily we can be led to provide ourselves with answers that are at complete odds with reality.

How can I live happily and excel? is the underlying question we are asking ourselves in every minute of every day. Our entire culture functions as a set of leading questions, and the seven rules are the wrong answers we're led to about how we can excel in our lives. If we truly want excellence we have to be willing to explore some alternatives other than being normal, avoiding mistakes, being independent, staying comfortable, pretending we don't matter, staying in control, and being popular. Such an exploration requires **Intelligent Misbehavior**, previously defined as the willingness to challenge hidden rules that compromise individual and organizational potential.

Intelligent Misbehavior requires a great amount of courage, since acting outside of the rules is not supported by our culture. If we want lasting change and sustainable success we will need to engage in ruthless self-examination. We will also need to take risks, surrender to our passion, exercise self-discipline, create a support network, and stick to our vision in the face of criticism. The necessity of **Intelligent Misbehavior** arises from our need to challenge our existing motivations, not to add new ones.

I once sat next to a man on a flight who shortly after take-off began telling me about his hunting hobby, in some degree of graphic detail. I casually mentioned to him that I was a vegetarian, and the guy didn't miss a beat. He just looked at me and said, "If God didn't want us to eat animals, he wouldn't have made them out of meat."

Living in denial of our self-justifications and arguing for our limitations may provide a chuckle when we see it from an outside perspective, but we must root out our own versions of twisted logic and our unthinking allegiances to flawed ideas before excellence can be restored.

If we are interested in rising to our full potential, then we have some difficult work to do. Fortunately, the challenges are balanced by equal and even greater rewards. Consistently practicing the seven actions of **Intelligent Misbehavior** will allow you to extricate yourself from the grip of our hidden rules and move more and more deeply into the life you were born to live. It will also make you a leader, able to support the organizations you most care about by being an example of appropriate rule breaking.

THE POWER OF STORIES, APPRECIATION, AND ACTION

BY THIS POINT IT'S OBVIOUS that I'm a firm believer in the power of stories. We can talk forever about the principles of excellence, but it is my experience that tangible examples help us a thousand-fold over theoretical discussions.

The power of stories rests in their ability to highlight and communicate values. When we lead our lives on the lookout for situations, occurrences, and individuals that embody the values we want to honor in our lives, we empower those values. They become magnified in our attention, and change begins to occur. Appreciation is one of the most important activities we can engage as we seek personal or organizational excellence.

Once we have recognized and appreciated the value of an idea, a person, a vision, or a practice, we are confronted with a crucial step. This is where you and I most often fall off the wagon in our quest for real change. I am, of course, talking about taking action. The seven rules all disable our ability to act. The only hope we have for transcending the dominance of these rules is to work slowly, consistently, and reliably with the **Actions of Intelligent Misbehavior** to reverse their grip.

There are three types of people reading this book. The first type will not see any value in these ideas and will forget them immediately. The second type of person will see their value clearly and immediately put them into practice.

Most of us, however, fall into the third category. We will see the value of such ideas and then entertain the thought that we will do something to put the recommended practices into play at some point in the future. This is a little trick many of us use to avoid change. We tell ourselves we're going to go back and apologize for an error, clean up our dirty dishes, or donate to a good cause we heard about, but we usually don't. It's an important thing to see about ourselves: that once we walk away from an opportunity to act, the likelihood of our going back is extremely low.

I live in a nice middle-class neighborhood. The local shops and stores near my home are mainly on one street, spanning about four long blocks and ranging from grocery stores to dentists to travel agencies to restaurants. All day long the residents of this quaint part of town come and go, shop and drive, eat and run.

I recently stopped and gave money to a beggar I've seen on this street for years but have previously ignored. He didn't ask me for money. In observing him over the past year I've come to realize something unusual about him, and I volunteered the donation because he inspired me. He has developed the habit of attending immediately to the details of his environment. He picks up trash and litter wherever he sees it, including items as small as a toothpick. He asks some of the merchants if he can borrow their broom and he sweeps their sidewalk. He pulls weeds out of the bordered garden areas that have been created along parts of the street. I've seen him cleaning around the edges of storefront windows with a toothbrush. He says hello to the people around him, smiles, and expresses cheerfulness.

This behavior is not unusual because this man is a street person. It's unusual, period, when anyone is willing to take responsibility for his or her immediate environment and for being in relationship to it through action, especially when those surroundings do not include one's own personal property.

This homeless person has developed the habit of responding to the present needs of his environment with action. His decision to consistently provide value to the merchants and residents of my local community now earns him donations of food, drink, and sometimes cash. But it didn't start this way. It took some significant period of time providing value without an expectation of return before the benefits started coming his way.

Here are three questions we can use as a reality check for how oriented we are to the essential spirit of action.

1. Do I have a vision for my own actions that makes them fulfilling enough that I would engage them without the need for any immediate acknowledgement or reward?

2. Do I act with faith that doing the right thing consistently over time will see me through?

3. Do I understand that I will discover possibilities in life as I move forward with committed action, not through gaining some guarantee of results *before* I move forward?

At first glance, we might see the apparently homeless or poor beggar in the above example as someone to be pitied, imagining that he is suffering. If my neighbors and I could see through his eyes, however, perhaps we would be surprised by how much he actually pities each of us, for most of us are poor in comparison to his focus, commitment, and freedom to serve.

In actuality, the greater suffering is sustained by those of us who recognize value and perceive need but, due to our obedience to the seven rules, refrain from taking action. We were born to give and create. We've been trained, however, to take and consume. We have the job of restoring our natural impulses to helpful, useful and sometimes even heroic actions instead of allowing those actions to remain trapped within us because we're unconsciously obeying rules.

Learning requires experience. The seven rules, however, are antiexperiential. When we obey any of them, we sideline ourselves and become passive spectators at the event we call our lives. Excellence requires our full and passionate participation at every stage.

If you recognize yourself in the rule-scripts I've outlined in this book and would like to take one simple step that could be the beginning of changing this habit forever, I recommend the following.

Red lipstick.

The first task is to find some, and then here's what you do with it. Walk into the bathroom or washroom in your home or workplace. Use the lipstick to write all seven of the misbehaviors of excellence on the bathroom mirror.

BE AUTHENTIC

TAKE CHANCES

ASK FOR HELP

BE DETERMINED

ACT IMPORTANT

BUILD RELATIONSHIPS

FOLLOW A VISION

Beneath this list, write the following final words.

PLEASE HELP ME REMEMBER TO ACT.

Then clearly sign your name with the lipstick.

With this single action, you will have broken every one of the seven rules.

1. This is obviously not a normal thing to do and represents an authentic interest in real change.

2. It's a risk and definitely qualifies as taking a chance. There is no way of knowing what might be set in motion by this simple action.

3. You've just asked openly for help. How other people may support you and to what extent will open a whole new possibility for both you and the individuals who respond.

4. You've committed an act of determination, which is often characterized by using creative means to achieve an objective.

5. You are standing for your significance and your ability to make a difference through tangible action.

6. The nature of your relationships to those who see the list will have the opportunity to deepen. Some of them will ask you questions, and it will be your chance to engage in a meaningful way with them.

7. You will have demonstrated your willingness to follow a vision that holds true potential.

This is only the beginning of your future as a joyous misbehaver. If you want to keep the door open to your newfound potential, take a picture of your mirror and send it to me at www.breakarule.com. I'll post your photo on the site as a reminder for you and as an inspiration to others.

While I've suggested that we have been disempowered as a

culture by a few unexamined rules, it's also true that inspiring examples of misbehavior are all around us. There are individuals that each of you knows who have broken these rules in both moving and spectacular ways. You also have stories from your own lives about successful rule breaking that others would benefit from hearing.

If you have found the material in this book to be of value, I urge you to get involved by sharing your own perspectives, your own wisdom, and your own immediate experience as a citizen of our culture. I'd love it if you'd send me a story of rule breaking or anything that inspires you to misbehave intelligently.

☆

Breakarule.com is the resource site for
7 Rules You Were Born to Break. Under the tab
"Tools for Breaking Rules" you'll find the contribution
center where you can share your own stories
of **Intelligent Misbehavior**.

I am no rule-breaking hero. The seven rules I've explored here are daily, even minute-to-minute, challenges that I personally face. Sometimes I overcome them; at other times I succumb to them. My hope is that by recording my thoughts and observations many conversations will be started among others and myself, and perhaps by groups of readers considering these ideas on their own, initiating conversations that spur increasingly intelligent, thoughtful lines of questioning and self-study that reawaken our inherent thirst for excellence.

May we all refuse to allow our passion to recede, to pretend that we are helpless, to act like we don't know what we should do. When we take responsibility for our illusions, it is only then that we connect to the truth that outshines them.

The truth beyond the seven rules is that we are born with clarity, radiance, and purpose. My hope is that by considering these ideas and joining forces we may live this truth more fully.

Appendix

TOOLS FOR
BREAKING RULES

THE MOTIVATIONAL SPEAKING INDUSTRY is famous for getting people excited and revved up in a meeting room, yet somehow the most inspiring of messages seem to gradually or sometimes immediately fade away once we're no longer within earshot of the speaker or as soon as the self-help book is finished and back on the shelf. As a presenter in this industry, I feel a very strong obligation to provide whatever tools and resources

I can to support sustainable change for the individuals and organizations with whom I work.

On my website at www.breakarule.com you will find Tools for Breaking Rules. Along with other resources and offerings there, you will find the Take AIM Training Program that has been designed to leverage as much benefit from the reading of this book as possible. It picks up where the book leaves off, offering next steps for anyone who has familiarized themselves with the core concepts and principles of **Intelligent Misbehavior** and who wishes to integrate new habits for achieving excellence into their daily life. An acronym for **Actions of Intelligent Misbehavior**, the Take AIM program is available to any owner of this book or to those who have attended one of my live presentations.

Once signed up, you will receive one e-mail a week in a 21-week follow-up training. Each mailing has been designed to help you integrate the **7 Actions of Intelligent Misbehavior** into daily life.

The training program is a dedicated practice field for AIM members where we will all have the opportunity to practice each of the misbehaviors: Be Authentic; Take Chances; Ask for Help; Be Determined; Act Important; Build Relationships; Follow a Vision.

I sincerely hope you'll join the AIM program. Your participation matters!

ACKNOWLEDGMENTS

I've come to the conclusion that individuals do not write good books. The worthwhile ones are written by an entire team of people who have supported the apparent author either directly in the writing process or along the way in the author's life. Without the direct help I received from my family, numerous supporters, and friends, this book would not exist. Nor could it have come into being without the direction and inspiration I've been fortunate to receive from many trainers, coaches, and mentors.

My deepest thanks goes to my teacher Lee, who demonstrates the practically perfect execution of all of these misbehaviors.

This project could not have been completed without the support of my wife Clelia, who has been my unfailing friend, loving companion, wise counselor, and frank mirror. Not only did she provide excellent and sometimes ruthless counsel in the early stages of this writing, she has consistently taken up the slack I left in our household life without judgment, resentment, or residue. Her loving-kindness melts me, leaves me in awe, and makes everything in our lives workable and possible.

My gratitude goes to my editor, Nancy Lewis, who fine-tuned this all the way through and whose input in the early stages of its writing pulled me out of many ditches that I'd still be sitting in if it weren't for her honesty and her commitment to the potential of the project. She has been nothing but patient, supportive, available, and reliable. I wish she were my mother. Oh yeah, she is.

A huge thanks to my longtime friend, master writer, and the world's greatest cheerleader, Red Hawk, who, with his accomplice Chandrika, gave me more motivation in the course of an hour to complete this project than everyone else combined.

I am extremely grateful for the input from my father, Richard, who read the manuscript with fresh eyes in its later stages and encouraged me to say just what is useful instead of everything I could think of. His counsel saved you from having to read double the existing number of pages to get the same content.

My father-in-law and retired English teacher, Bob Krieckhaus, came to the rescue when I needed to make sure the ideas and my communication of them were logically sound. His astute comments and willingness to think deeply about these principles helped me to clarify sloppy thought and weed out inaccuracies and to pay attention to my reader's experience.

Thanks to my friend Tom Shelby, who dedicated some of the little sleep time he has left in his life to reading the manuscript in its final stage and for having the courage to offer great suggestions and improvements even after I thought the book was done.

Gwyn Morgan, founding CEO of Encana Corp., generously read this manuscript at my request and offered some detailed and hard-hitting feedback that improved the final draft immeasurably. I was touched and impressed by his willingness to give this project thoughtful attention in the midst of his many other responsibilities and duties.

Thanks to Regina Sara Ryan, senior editor at Hohm Press, for her support and encouragement to write and for sharing the wisdom of her experience in the creation of books.

Thanks to Dasya and Joe Zuccarello at One World Press for the many conversations I had with each of them that moved this project forward and for the usefulness of their personal and professional counsel.

I'm greatly appreciative to Kim Johansen, owner of Black Dog Design, for really listening to what I wanted in the book's design and rising to its significant challenge with her creative talents. She carefully considered my market, what would be best for the book on numerous levels, and went beyond the call of duty in service to the project.

Thanks to my speaking agent, Christa Haberstock, for supporting my vision and patiently waiting for me to get this right. Thanks to Ari for believing in Christa's vision and serving it so capably.

SEO mentor Michael Linehan of Marketing Alchemy years ago lent me an important piece of writing he had done on the essentials of business development. It turned my thinking around and helped me clarify what I am really here to do as a presenter for special events, ultimately helping to pave the way to the creation of this book. Thanks also to Ken Lapp of Standard Marketing for his professionalism and integrity while supporting me with the development of my online marketing material.

Thanks to Sean Hern, John Smith, and Lisa Turner for their understanding of my process and for giving me the chance to model something positive to my children and to lay the foundation for a brighter future for my family in a challenging time.

While this book uses no footnotes or direct quotations from other sources, I am indebted to many inspiring practitioners of excellence and champions of the human spirit for many of its core ideas. In addition to the unfailing example of my teacher, Lee Lozowick, and his teacher, Indian saint Yogi Ramsuratkumar, I am grateful to have experienced the Landmark Forum and the work of Werner Erhard, and thankful for the mentorship, guidance, and friendship of Purna Steinitz and my experiences with The Event.

I have used the writings and practical, no-nonsense guidance of sales master Jeffrey Gitomer without ever meeting him. His example of the difference an individual can make through a commitment to the writing process inspired me to stick with my own writing practice.

The work of Gordon Neufeld in relationship to child development had an important influence on my ideas around growth for adults and has been of great help with my real-life parenting.

My children Nate, Ruby, and Aditya inspire me, astound me, keep me on the ground, remind me how to be, and make me a proud and happy dad. Thanks to Nate for pursuing his passion. Thanks to Ruby, who composed and gave me this thoughtful quote as I was working to complete the book: "The ultimate experience comes from what we dare to be."

Jim Farkus, a member of the Hungarian Olympic gymnastic

team and founder of the United States Gymnastics Federation, taught me the necessity of discipline and made a powerful impression on me as a boy. Lorraine Cranford, the founder of Ballet Arkansas, taught me how to be precise. Theater director Rand Hopkins taught me the power of enthusiasm.

As noted in the manuscript, the faculty at Webster University inspired me and armed me with tools for growth and personal development that were irreplaceable. I give special thanks to Sue Ott Rowlands, Sarah Barker, Rick Ericson, and Gavin Cameron-Webb.

Thanks to Amy Maguire for truth seeking with me in the early years and sharing a love for the power of words.

Thanks to all our wonderful dear friends in Arizona who helped us pack and move all our stuff in a stressful time and who are the reason we still call Arizona home. We miss you all.

I'm grateful for my close friend Geoff Carr, who has been there for me in every way through the triumphs and challenges of many years and whose company I so enjoy. I appreciate his wisdom and his commitment to his own personal work as he dedicates himself to helping others in his counseling practice.

Thanks to high school friends George Newbern and Skip Lackey for being steady and solid over time and distance.

Thanks also to PJ Reece for his longstanding friendship and the wise words he has shared at just the right times about fatherhood.

Eric Brummel has been my companion in big thinking and has inspired me to stop playing small by taking risks and being inventive in his own work helping others through his physical therapy business.

My gratitude to the speaking and entertainment agencies that have believed in me over the years and used me for their customers, especially John Kelly, David Richardson, Dave Vandiver, and John Sykes. And thanks to speaker Robert Stevenson for his encouragement and introduction years ago to the speaking industry.

Thanks to my brother Jeff and his wife Terri for caring about family.

Lisa Bagshaw deserves great credit for traveling to the other side of the world into the unknown with nothing but a tent, a bicycle, and a street juggler.

My gratitude goes to all those street performers who have dedicated themselves to an art form that becomes more difficult with each passing year. I thank all street performers for keeping an important tradition alive and for experimenting, taking risks, pushing the envelope, making people laugh, provoking thoughtfulness, and engaging other human beings in real life.

I give my thanks to the million or so folks over the years who have given me the privilege of their attention while I experimented with humor and rule breaking. I am especially grateful to all those audience volunteers who have participated in my performances and routines.

Finally, I'd like to thank in advance all those readers of this book who will make the effort to participate in rule breaking and especially to those who contribute their own stories of **Intelligent Misbehavior** to a budding generation of rule breakers.

LaVergne, TN USA
17 August 2010
193500LV00001B/17/P